ADVANCE PRAISE FOR *A Cry in Unison*

A Cry in Unison, by Judy Weissenberg Cohen, is a sweeping memoir of Holocaust history, filled with memories of a happy childhood in a large and loving extended family, vignettes of mischievous behaviour, stories illustrating a love of family and Jewish culture, and descriptions of a life drastically changed by the Nazi occupation. Judy's account of Auschwitz-Birkenau is of "one heart-stopping event after another." Through her eyes, we see the surrogate family she created — the "camp sisters" with whom she faced starvation, sickness and cruelty. Judy also writes about her postwar journey and her struggles as a refugee in Canada, portraying in detail the slow and often painful process of adaptation. As Judy tries to acclimate to life in Montreal and Toronto, there are moments for laughter as well as for tears.

I've known Judy since she approached me for permission to use my articles about women's experiences during the Holocaust on her website, a site that has grown into an important resource for this work on Jewish women's lives. Now, her memoir adds to that body of knowledge. Judy's optimistic and vivacious personality shines through her writing, as does her strong and indomitable spirit. She shares with us a painful story of survival under the worst imaginable conditions, engaging us with her energy, sincerity and sensitivity, letting us feel her love of life despite the horrors she witnessed and experienced. *A Cry in Unison* invites us to witness the worst of humanity and, in doing so, warns us of the cost of indifference and hatred. It is one of the most informative and heart-rending accounts I have read.

Dr. Myrna Goldenberg, co-editor of *Different Horrors, Same Hell: Gender and the Holocaust* and editor of *Before All Memory Is Lost: Women's Voices from the Holocaust*

When I first met Judy Weissenberg Cohen at a Holocaust conference many years ago, I was immediately struck by her sharp and fearless curiosity. Her questions and comments were grounded in the intelligence of her heart. *A Cry in Unison* not only recounts the author's own story of survival during the Holocaust but also provides us with the powerful account of a woman rising beyond victimhood to become a strong voice advocating for social justice. This much-anticipated memoir is indispensable for the study of women and the Holocaust. Judy Weissenberg Cohen has something important to say to you, dear reader.

> *Dr. Sonja M. Hedgepeth*, co-editor of *Sexual Violence against Jewish Women during the Holocaust*

Judy Weissenberg Cohen has written a compelling memoir that eloquently weaves together personal experience with social and political realities. She masterfully shares her history by offering unique insights, supported by a strong gender analysis. *A Cry in Unison* is framed by meticulous research that enables the reader to situate private experience within a wide scope, enabling a fully nuanced story to emerge. Her words recalling the past invoke an urgent warning for the present.

> *Dr. Joan Simalchik*, Director, Women and Gender Studies Program, University of Toronto Mississauga

I have admired Judy Weissenberg Cohen's work on women and the Holocaust for two decades. She has been on the advisory board of Remember the Women Institute, an organization dedicated to including women's stories in Holocaust history, since soon after our inception in 1997. Her website, Women and the Holocaust — a Cyberspace of Their Own, has been an invaluable teaching tool and has been cited in scholarly works. Likewise, her memoir is more than a memoir because her memories of the Holocaust are backed up with historical material and footnotes.

Unlike many Holocaust survivors, Judy Cohen has never been hesitant to discuss sexual violence. When Dr. Sonja M. Hedgepeth and I edited our 2010 book on the subject, *Sexual Violence against Jewish Women during the Holocaust*, we interviewed Judy and used some of her remarks in our introduction, and she spoke openly and honestly about sexual violence. I am grateful for her wisdom and for her clear recollections about her experiences during the Holocaust, and especially for the publication of her memoir. Judy has always asked, "Where are the women?" and continues to do so. By telling her story, Judy helps to fill this gap in history.

Dr. Rochelle G. Saidel, Founder and Executive Director, Remember the Women Institute

A Cry in Unison is not just the story of a Hungarian survivor of Auschwitz-Birkenau. Although Judy Cohen's wartime experiences are its focus, the memoir also tells the story of someone who has spent the last two decades fighting antisemitism and Holocaust denial and supporting Holocaust education in Canada.

As an adolescent in the Nazi camps, where she experienced one unimaginable situation after another, Judy found a sense of protection in the bonds she had with her sisters and fellow prisoners. After the Holocaust, Judy did not forget her murdered family members, but her memories of the love and support she felt growing up empowered her, and Judy was able to find meaning in her life and create her own family. On one hand, Judy's narrative speaks to the agency people have in determining their own fate, yet it also recognizes how luck determines matters of life and death. Judy's memoir recounts all those moments — those she fell victim to and those she tried to control.

After I met Judy at a workshop about women and the Holocaust that Lenore Weitzman and I organized in 1996, and following the publication of the book *Women in the Holocaust* in 1998, Judy launched a website publishing academic articles on the topic, including my own. The site has been a great contribution to spreading awareness and knowledge of the experience of women during those difficult times, and after reading her memoir, my appreciation of Judy has developed into a deep admiration of her and her work.

Dr. Dalia Ofer, (Emerita) The Avraham Harman Institute of Contemporary Jewry and the Department of Jewish History, The Hebrew University of Jerusalem

A Cry in Unison

THE AZRIELI SERIES OF HOLOCAUST SURVIVOR MEMOIRS: PUBLISHED TITLES

ENGLISH TITLES

A Cry in Unison:
Sistering for Survival

Judy Weissenberg Cohen

THE AZRIELI FOUNDATION · www.azrielifoundation.org

Cover image by Raphael Mohar. "The Last Ones in the Bunker," 1946. Courtesy of Ghetto Fighters' House Museum, Israel/Photo Archive
Cover design by Endpaper Studio
Book design by Mark Goldstein
Map on page xxxiii by Deborah Crowle
Endpaper maps by Martin Gilbert
Family Tree on pages xxxiv–xxxv by Keaton Taylor

LIBRARY AND ARCHIVES CANADA CATALOGUING IN PUBLICATION

A cry in unison: sistering for survival / Judy Weissenberg Cohen.

Cohen, Judy Weissenberg, 1928– author. Azrieli Foundation, publisher.
Azrieli series of Holocaust survivor memoirs. Series XII
Canadiana 20200213989 · ISBN 9781988065700 (softcover) · 8 7 6 5 4 3 2 1

LCSH: Cohen, Judy Weissenberg, 1928– LCSH: Holocaust, Jewish (1939–1945) — Hungary — Personal narratives. LCSH: Holocaust, Jewish (1939-1945) — Personal narratives. LCSH: Jewish women — Hungary — Biography. LCSH: Jewish women — Canada — Biography. LCSH: Jews — Hungary — Biography. LCSH: Jews — Canada — Biography. LCSH: Holocaust survivors — Canada — Biography. LC-GFT: Autobiographies. LCGFT: Personal narratives.

LCC DS135.H93 C64 2020 · DDC 940.53/18092 — DC23

MIX
Paper from
responsible sources
FSC
www.fsc.org   FSC® C004191

PRINTED IN CANADA

The Azrieli Foundation's Holocaust Survivor Memoirs Program

Naomi Azrieli, Publisher

Jody Spiegel, Program Director
Arielle Berger, Managing Editor
Matt Carrington, Editor
Devora Levin, Editor and Special Projects Coordinator
Elizabeth Lasserre, Senior Editor, French-Language Editions
Elin Beaumont, Community and Education Initiatives
Catherine Person, Education and Academic Initiatives/French Editor
Stephanie Corazza, Academic and Education Initiatives
Marc-Olivier Cloutier, School and Education Initiatives
Elizabeth Banks, Digital Asset Curator and Archivist
Catherine Quintal, Digital Communications Assistant

Mark Goldstein, Art Director
François Blanc, Cartography Advisor
Bruno Paradis, Layout, French-Language Editions

Contents

Series Preface:
In their own words...

In telling these stories, the writers have liberated themselves. For so many years we did not speak about it, even when we became free people living in a free society. Now, when at last we are writing about what happened to us in this dark period of history, knowing that our stories will be read and live on, it is possible for us to feel truly free. These unique historical documents put a face on what was lost, and allow readers to grasp the enormity of what happened to six million Jews — one story at a time.

> David J. Azrieli, C.M., C.Q., M.Arch
> Holocaust survivor and founder, The Azrieli Foundation

Since the end of World War II, approximately 40,000 Jewish Holocaust survivors have immigrated to Canada. Who they are, where they came from, what they experienced and how they built new lives for themselves and their families are important parts of our Canadian heritage. The Azrieli Foundation's Holocaust Survivor Memoirs Program was established in 2005 to preserve and share the memoirs written by those who survived the twentieth-century Nazi genocide of the Jews of Europe and later made their way to Canada. The memoirs encourage readers to engage thoughtfully and critically with the complexities of the Holocaust and to create meaningful connections with the lives of survivors.

Millions of individual stories are lost to us forever. By preserving the stories written by survivors and making them widely available to a broad audience, the Azrieli Foundation's Holocaust Survivor Memoirs Program seeks to sustain the memory of all those who perished at the hands of hatred, abetted by indifference and apathy. The personal accounts of those who survived against all odds are as different as the people who wrote them, but all demonstrate the courage, strength, wit and luck that it took to prevail and survive in such terrible adversity. The memoirs are also moving tributes to people — strangers and friends — who risked their lives to help others, and who, through acts of kindness and decency in the darkest of moments, frequently helped the persecuted maintain faith in humanity and courage to endure. These accounts offer inspiration to all, as does the survivors' desire to share their experiences so that new generations can learn from them.

The Holocaust Survivor Memoirs Program collects, archives and publishes select survivor memoirs and makes the print editions available free of charge to educational institutions and Holocaust-education programs across Canada. They are also available for sale online to the general public. All revenues to the Azrieli Foundation from the sales of the Azrieli Series of Holocaust Survivor Memoirs go toward the publishing and educational work of the memoirs program.

∼

The Azrieli Foundation would like to express appreciation to the following people for their invaluable efforts in producing this book: Doris Bergen, Mark Duffus (Maracle Inc.), Jane Pavanel, Susan Roitman, Stephen Ullstrom, and Margie Wolfe & Emma Rodgers of Second Story Press. A special thank you to Bev Birkan, who listened to Judy's story and helped her begin writing her memoir.

About the Footnotes and Glossary

The following memoir contains a number of terms, concepts and historical references that may be unfamiliar to the reader. The editor has added footnotes relevant to the memoir, and explanations of some terms were generated from the Azrieli Foundation's extensive glossary. For general information on major organizations; significant historical events and people; geographical locations; religious and cultural terms; and foreign-language words and expressions that will help give context and background to the events described in the text, please see the glossary beginning on page 135.

Introduction

I first met Judy — I am using her first name here with affection because I have come to know her well, academically and personally — at a conference on Holocaust education, which she attended as the founder of the website Women and the Holocaust — a Cyberspace of Their Own. She established this site in 2001, before it became prevalent in the field of Holocaust studies to consider women's experiences specifically. It was not long before this that the distinguished professor of Holocaust studies Carol Rittner had famously asked her colleague John Roth, after reading his 1989 book on the Holocaust, "Where are the women?" Rittner then set to the task of filling this gap with *Different Voices: Women and the Holocaust*, a seminal volume containing the work of pioneering scholars of women's Holocaust experiences, co-edited with Roth and published in 1993. Michelle, Judy's daughter, thoughtfully offered her mother a copy of the book, and it had a profound impact on her.

At the time that Judy began learning about Holocaust scholarship in the 1990s, there was a belief among many researchers and survivors that Jewish suffering during the German Judeocide should not be differentiated by gender or age so as not to lose sight of the horrors perpetrated against all Jews. Therefore, this new cognizance of women's experiences in the Holocaust frequently met with resistance. Yet, as Judy explains in her memoir, the aim of this scholarship was not to efface men's suffering, but to highlight that women were often treated differently on account of their gender and their status in family life and in society as a whole.

With the help of her son, Jonathan, Judy began using the internet in the 1990s, daring to venture into the world of technology as a senior. Echoing Rittner, Judy asked the editor of the Holocaust website remember.org, "And where are the women on your website?" She then set out to become a digital collector of female voices, as well as of writings based on research about women's specific experiences in the Holocaust. Judy describes her path to creating her website with passion. She felt compelled to bring both academia and personal reflections to a much wider audience, and over the years many educators and students have indeed found guidance and source material through her site. The regularly updated bibliographies are inclusive in that texts by or about women are marked with an asterisk and do not form a separate category. Judy's website is a significant example of her persistent efforts to help chart a new course in studying and teaching the Holocaust.

For years, Judy was busy giving talks at conferences and networking with scholars and survivors, inviting them to contribute to her site and becoming a connector and facilitator who brought researchers together and widened the scope of Holocaust education. She even travelled as far as Israel to attend presentations at the biennial conference on women and the Holocaust and to engage in discussions with scholars and survivors. I saw her there and at many such places. Judy came to meet me at the 2017 Congress of Humanities and Social Sciences at Ryerson University carrying a copy of the latest book by Dr. Myrna Goldenberg, which the author had intended for me. Even though Judy was using a walker, she did not mind travelling the distance as a "mailwoman." It pleased her that she could contribute to the sharing of research, even if it was by personally delivering a new book on women in the Holocaust. She was still tireless, even though, in the previous few years, she had been in ill health and weighed down by the mental and physical burden of attending to her husband, who has since passed away.

Although Judy Cohen had been collecting women's Holocaust stories for decades, one account was missing — her own. She had published a few of her memories over the years on her website: in 1999, "Fräulein," about the moment of liberation, followed by her moving piece, "A Most Memorable Kol Nidre," in the same year. In 2004, her article "March 19, 1944: A fateful day for Hungarian Jews" was published in the *Canadian Jewish News*. All three pivotal memories are included under the section "Fragments" on her site. Now, after years of speaking, facilitating and sharing her own and others' testimonies, she has decided to publish her complete story.

∼

Judy Cohen's family lived in Debrecen, Hungary's second-largest city after Budapest, situated in the northeast of the country. As the tide of war changed in 1944–1945, it briefly became the capital of Hungary. While overtly antisemitic laws began to affect Jewish Germans when Hitler came to power in 1933, Hungary had been the first country to curtail the civil rights of Jews by introducing a 6 per cent student quota, *numerus clausus,* in higher education in 1920. This law introduced the idea of Jews as a separate nationality from the rest of the population, although the concept of a "Jewish nationality" had not existed in Hungarian law. The *numerus clausus* law had a deleterious effect on many Jewish families whose members were expelled from universities, including the University of Debrecen, the oldest continuously operating institution of higher education in the country. An amendment to that law, which eliminated differentiation by nationality or religion, was introduced in 1928 because of international pressure. But the Second Anti-Jewish Law, passed by the Hungarian parliament under Miklós Horthy in 1939, reintroduced the legal distinction between Jews and Hungarian citizens, this time defining Jews as a distinct "race," a definition that was akin to the 1935

Nazi race laws of Nuremberg. Jews' access to universities and certain professions such as law, government administration and journalism, as well as some commercial and industrial enterprises, was limited. More anti-Jewish edicts followed.

Judy's large family felt the effects of Hungary's anti-Jewish measures that were introduced in the late 1930s. Two of Judy's siblings, Klári and Laci, were not allowed to attend a state university and had to go to work instead. Young Judy was forbidden from attending a regular high school.

Although widespread public and official antisemitism continued to affect Hungary's Jews, often in the form of aggressive demonstrations or individual attacks, many still believed that this onerous situation would not last. They had every reason to think that they were an integral part of their country, citizens first and Jews second. Hungary was their homeland to which they were bound linguistically and culturally, while contributing to the country's economy and raising their children as Hungarian citizens.

However, the persecution of Hungary's Jews continued and intensified. In November 1940, just over a year after the onset of World War II, Hungary became an ideological and military ally of Nazi Germany. That year, Judy's father, Sándor Weissenberg, was forced to close down his business, directly impacted by new anti-Jewish regulations. Like so many other Jewish fathers at that time, he lost his ability to provide for his family, and with it his pride.

But the biggest change for Judy and her family happened four years later:

Our lives immediately and profoundly changed on March 19, 1944. When the Nazis became aware that Hungary wanted to withdraw from the Axis alliance and that Miklós Horthy was making overtures to the Allies, the German army marched into Hungary and occupied it, with SS officer Adolf Eichmann in charge of ghettoizing and deporting the Jews. Matters proceeded with lightning speed.... My memories of that time are of constantly worried faces and whispered discussions among the adults around us. The children absorbed their grave concerns by osmosis, and our childhoods were not allowed to blossom as we lived with uncertainty from day to day.

From April 1944 on, Hungarian Jews were required to wear a yellow Star of David on their clothes in public, as had been decreed in an edict dated March 31. Germany had started this public identification of Jews with the *Judenstern*, "Jewish star," when they invaded Poland in 1939 and demanded that countries under their control identify Jews in this way. The yellow stars have become a well-known symbol of the Holocaust, but what did they mean for the people who had to wear them? Judy applies contemporary terminology to her experience when she says that the Jews became a "visible minority." She relates how she would cover up the badge with books that she held in front of her in what she calls "my little act of resistance."

Soon after this edict, Hungarian Jews were forced to live in overcrowded ghettos before being sent to death camps, mainly Auschwitz-Birkenau. Judy writes about the ghetto not only in terms of the hopelessness there but also about herself as part of a community, a theme that emerges throughout her memoir.

Judy remembers Thursday, June 29, 1944, the day of the dreaded deportation, and the "Hungarian soldiers pushing and shoving people into the cattle cars." The Weissenberg family was among the 430,000 Hungarian Jews who were taken away for what was euphemistically called "resettlement," *Umsiedlung,* or simply "transport." Few thought that they would be killed. The Nazis, with the collaboration and support of the Hungarians, sent 147 trains, each carrying 3,000 Hungarian Jews, daily to Auschwitz-Birkenau from mid-May to mid-July of 1944. Most were killed immediately. Under international pressure, the Hungarian government halted deportations on July 6, 1944, but in spite of these orders, additional trains of victims continued to be sent to Auschwitz.

The Nazis had even calculated the cost and profit of these trains and their cargo, weighing the cost of the transports against the profit they would get from the Jews' confiscated property. Human beings and goods became equal, and mere statistics. Judy gives us an indication of the horrid conditions on the train, a glimpse into a world that was unimaginable, one that she says is "impossible to adequately describe."

Yet, Judy does vividly describe images from Birkenau and other hellholes created by the Germans, where she was the recipient of and witness to beastly treatment and utter viciousness. Upon arrival at the death camp there was the "selection," or *Selektion*, an infamous and horrible fact of this place. Officials waved the dumbfounded people either to the left or right. Little did the victims know that one of those directions meant immediate death by gassing. Judy and her three older sisters were lucky, initially at least, to be on the path to survival together. Her writing underlines the importance of a support group — "sistering," as she calls it — even with non-family members, as was later the case. Suffering became communal, a significant factor that has been cited in other accounts by women who talk about their survival of the Nazi death camps.

The title of Judy's memoir, *A Cry in Unison*, represents this idea of shared agony with a circle of women in captivity. Her moving account of 1999, "A Most Memorable Kol Nidre," presented as the prologue here, is perhaps the best illustration. She recounts how hundreds of women in Birkenau "burst out in a cry — in unison" as one woman began to recite the Kol Nidre prayer on the most solemn of Jewish holidays, Yom Kippur. As Judy says, this "heart-rending sound" has stayed with her all her life. At the time, this gathering strengthened both the individual and the group; her pain was at one with the pain of the others, and they could all take comfort in knowing that nobody was alone.

Italian Auschwitz survivor Primo Levi famously wrote about how chances of survival in the death camps were better if one understood what was being said in that dangerous environment. Judy had learned German early on at the Jewish parochial school in Debrecen and at home, and it likely helped her deal with critical situations while in German captivity. However, the German spoken in the death camps was not what inmates had learned at school or from their parents, guardians or nannies. The language used in the German concentration camps and in National Socialist Germany in general, since known as Nazi German or *Nazi-Deutsch*, is a complex and multifaceted construct that fills an entire book I co-authored with Robert Michael, *An English Lexicon of the Language of the Third Reich*. Throughout this expansive work of 6,500 entries, the Nazis' preoccupation with the Jews, their persecution and eventual annihilation, is mirrored in language. There is hardly a page without a reference to the murder of Jews. It begins with "A" as the abbreviation of *Arbeitsjuden* (Jews capable of work, to be worked to death) and ends with Zyklon-B (the deadly cyanide gas that was used to asphyxiate Jewish men, women and children).

Many survivors like Judy remember these and other German terms. She recalls that "loud screaming by the Lager leaders of 'Achtung! Achtung!' (Attention! Attention!) always sent shivers down our spines and inevitably meant selections, the most gut-wrenching times, worse even than hunger." She also recalls the *Zählappell*, roll call, part of daily life at Auschwitz-Birkenau, regardless of the weather, and conducted with such abuse that it became "a torture in itself." These and other German words have remained in Judy's consciousness and cannot adequately be translated because the translations could never carry the words' true meaning or reflect her experience. The Holocaust universe was the context for this language and there was no other.

Many survivors are haunted by the memory of the German expletives that Nazis used against incarcerated Jews, reducing the victims to objects. In fact, the Jews in the Nazi camps were even referred to as "pieces," *Stücke*, along with, as Judy mentions, *verfluchte*

Juden, accursed Jews, or *dreckige Juden*, dirty Jews. Abusive speech compounded the agony further for those already dying or trying to survive in abject conditions. To the killers, the word *Jude*, Jew, itself had become a degrading form of address, starting in Nazi Germany in the 1930s. Instead of using "Mr." when addressing Jewish men in German society, Nazi officials would use "Jew." In survivors' accounts we often find German invectives, often untranslated, because only in the original language could they carry their devastating force and import. Judy's memoir is no exception, and it contains a number of German words that have stayed with her all her life, unchanged.

One German word that Judy remembers is particularly revealing. Judy was on what was later called a "death march" — called so because for so many it meant death from exhaustion, hunger, illness or by physical violence or shooting. In retrospect, we know these marches were, for those who lived, the way to liberation, but at the time, there seemed no end in sight but oblivion. For Judy "the hunger was unbearable, relentless." But on the morning of Saturday, May 5, 1945, Judy awoke to hear the entire group of women she was with being addressed as *Fräulein*, "Ladies." She did not need a keen ear to distinguish the linguistic and tonal nuance of this word. After all the curses and ill-treatment, this German official had changed his tune, literally overnight. The reason was that he knew of the Allies' imminent arrival, signalling the end of the war. "It was a beautiful sunny day," Judy remembers poignantly, animating for the reader these long days of hardship and fear of death.

Eventually Judy returned to Hungary — a trip that she had anticipated with apprehension. Was this to be the termination of her dark journey? It may seem to outsiders that survival itself was the happy ending after the Holocaust. But for Judy and many others, arriving in their homeland meant unexpected situations and problems. There was surprise and hostility from neighbours when they saw that Jews had survived — they feared having to return the Jewish belongings they had unlawfully seized and they dreaded reprisals — all mixed in with the still present baseline antisemitism. In other European countries, Jewish survivors faced persecution, attacks, murders and actual pogroms. The situation in Hungary was a bit less severe than in Poland, where the number of Jewish victims after the Holocaust is estimated at two thousand. But still, approximately one hundred Jews were murdered upon their return to Hungary.

After Judy arrived back in Debrecen, in August 1945, she desperately wanted to know who from her family had survived and who had perished. From her immediate family, she met only her brother Laci. Judy went back to school, which was "a good distraction from wrestling with my agonizing memories and traumatic experiences." Like other Holocaust survivors, Judy had difficulty picking up the pieces of a shattered life in a place that did not feel like home any longer. In order to somehow continue, the trauma and the memories were repressed. But they were not forgotten. Judy and her brother soon learned that their sister Évi had survived as well but did not want to return to Hungary, and so Judy reluctantly left school and the three surviving siblings reunited in the Bergen-Belsen DP camp in Germany. Most importantly, they pondered how to move on, wanting to find a direction and a goal to pursue.

Judy forged ahead with courage and determination and eventually started life in a new country, Canada, and in a different language. On June 11, 1948, she arrived in Halifax at Pier 21, the entry point that became famous because so many new immigrants and refugees landed there. What did the new country have to offer her and other survivors? For one, it was a land at peace, and living here meant living in safety, without dreading the anticipated knock on the door, the hostility of the immediate environment or sudden laws that would take away their freedom. For refugees, these were important and essential factors. Yes, there were problems here too, and as Judy writes, "life wasn't always smooth sailing." Some difficulties were compounded by the fact that she had had a grim past and an upbringing in another country and at a different time. With candour she recounts downfalls and disappointments as she adjusted to life in a new country.

Judy was eager to become a member of the Canadian workforce, and after working in the garment industry she eventually took a business course and found jobs in bookkeeping and real estate. She married a good man, Sidney Cohen, and they raised two children. The family went on camping trips and bought a cottage, like other Canadians. For them, Canada offered natural beauty and healthy outdoor activities, yet the past was never far away. Judy could not forget what had happened to her and millions of other Jews in those traumatic years, and her desire for learning about the past would not diminish.

Shortly after an encounter with a group of Holocaust deniers in 1993, Judy retired. Shortly after that, she visited the Holocaust Centre of Toronto, wanting to help combat what she calls "this emerging assault on the Holocaust and historical truth." This was a big undertaking, and the start of a new and meaningful phase in Judy's life. Guided by her heart and a passion for the truth, she applied herself and started to read intently. The fact that the book before you includes a quasi-bibliography of her private study materials attests to the depth of Judy's quest. She wanted to understand the many unfathomable and perplexing events that lay beneath the decisions and actions of the Holocaust perpetrators as well as the experiences of its victims. What perhaps gave even more meaning to her studies was reading about women's "immense suffering and struggle to survive in the very places I also knew intimately."

Since her retirement, Judy has dedicated her time and energy to fulfill a commitment she made to teaching about the Holocaust. She particularly wanted to reach out to students, and she worked through her exhaustion, always accepting yet another invitation to address a class. She also participated in March of the Living four times, accompanying Jewish high school and college youth to Auschwitz and then Israel as a survivor who could speak to the truth about what had happened.

For Judy and many survivors, telling their story, or writing it down, is often a difficult and perilous task. How can they deal with the powerful memories that are etched in their hearts? Perhaps for Judy one way has been through acquiring background knowledge, which has given her the ability to situate the individual in the larger frame of history. For example, when she writes about her three brothers who were conscripted into the Hungarian army's forced labour battalions, along with tens of thousands of other Jewish men, she weaves in the facts she learned postwar: "Fifty thousand Jewish forced labourers were sent to the Eastern Front, into Soviet Ukraine with the Hungarian Second Army in 1942, and fewer than ten thousand would return." By inserting succinct historical-political facts throughout her memoir, Judy focuses on her story within the greater historical picture.

A desire to acquire knowledge, to learn, is a notable strand that winds itself through the narrative of Judy's life, and one of Judy's strengths. Although she was denied access to regular high school as Hungary applied antisemitic laws in the 1930s and 1940s, and the Holocaust, which ruptured her life and scarred her forever, prevented her from even thinking of a normal education, the life trajectory that Judy shares with us, from Hungary to Canada, is one that highlights education. Her learning and understanding of the history that lay at the bottom of Germany's intent to annihilate Jewish life in Europe, together with her own lived experiences, ultimately turned into the ability to educate others.

No two survivors' accounts are the same, even though there may be many parallels between them. Judy's book reveals the uniqueness of her decisions and character. We see her as a fighter, but she never paints herself as a heroine. She has been exceptionally courageous. She once told me that since her experiences in the Holocaust, she is not scared of anything, and to this day, Judy is not afraid to speak out. Those who know her are familiar with her engagement with injustices at home and abroad. She is always concerned about human rights violations or signs of genocidal tendencies. She has called out hate speech, antisemitic or otherwise, because she has experienced how words can turn into violent actions. She knows all too well that language matters. It has saddened and angered her, as it has many Holocaust survivors, that individuals and governments sometimes do not seem to have learned much from the history of genocide and from personal experiences with discrimination and murderous persecution.

Over the years, I have admired Judy's perseverance and diligence, and I am happy now that she has applied these admirable traits to writing her own story. Seeing her testimonial in front of me fills me with gladness that she has finally joined many other Holocaust survivors, particularly women, who have recounted their gender-specific experiences, which she so fervently sought to collect on her website. This remarkable achievement is an important part of her legacy, and *A Cry in Unison*, as her final contribution, reaches out to us with a story that illustrates the wide-ranging scope of this man-made catastrophe of the twentieth century, one that goes beyond the self, but of which she has been a part.

Before Judy takes us back to that past with her particular recollections, I think it poignant to end with a sentiment she always emphasizes to her audiences, which she also emphasizes in this memoir: "not to cry about my sad story but to *think* about the important issues I raised."

Karin Doerr, PhD
Simone de Beauvoir Institute and
Dept. of Modern Languages and Linguistics
Concordia University, Montreal
2020

SOURCES

Baer, Elizabeth R. and Myrna Goldenberg, eds. *Experience and Expression: Women, the Nazis, and the Holocaust.* Detroit: Wayne State University Press, 2003.

Bergen, Doris L. *War and Genocide: A Concise History of the Holocaust.* 3rd ed. New York: Rowman & Littlefield, 2002.

Doerr, Karin. "Words of Fear and Fear of Words: Language Memories of Holocaust Survivors." *vis-à-vis: Explorations in Anthropology,* special issue, Subjects of Fear 9, no. 1 (2009): 47–57.

Goldenberg, Myrna, ed. *Before All Memory Is Lost: Women's Voices from the Holocaust.* Toronto: The Azrieli Foundation, 2017.

Goldenberg, Myrna and Amy H. Shapiro, eds. *Different Horrors, Same Hell: Gender and the Holocaust.* Seattle: University of Washington Press, 2013.

Hass, Aaron. *The Aftermath: Living with the Holocaust.* New York: Cambridge University Press, 1995.

Hilberg, Raul. *The Role of the German Railroads in the Destruction of the Jews.* Washington, DC: American Sociological Association, 1976.

Hurshell, Patricia. *When Silence Speaks, When Women Sorrow: Rue and Difference in the Lamentation for the Six Million.* PhD diss., University of Washington, 1992.

Karady, Victor and Peter Tibor Nagy, eds. *The numerus clausus in Hungary: Studies on the First Anti-Jewish Law and Academic Anti-Semitism in Modern Central Europe.* Budapest: Pasts Inc. Centre for Historical Research, History Department of the Central European University, 2012.

Kertész, Imre. *Fateless.* Translated by Christopher C. and Katharina M. Wilson. Evanston, IL: Northwestern University Press, 1992.

Klemperer, Victor. *The Language of the Third Reich: LTI: Lingua Tertii Imperii: A Philologist's Notebook.* Translated by Martin Brady. London: Athlone Press, 2000.

Kluger, Ruth. *Still Alive: A Holocaust Girlhood Remembered.* Foreword by Lore Segal. New York: The Feminist Press, 2001.

Michael, Robert and Karin Doerr. *Nazi-Deutsch/Nazi German: An English Lexicon of the Language of the Third Reich.* Newport, CT: Greenwood Press, 2002.

Oore, Irene. *The Listener: In the Shadow of the Holocaust.* Regina, SA: Regina University Press, 2019.

Rittner, Carol and John K. Roth, eds. *Different Voices: Women and the Holocaust.* Westport, CT: Greenwood Press, 1997.

Yahil, Leni. *The Holocaust: The Fate of European Jewry, 1932–1945.* Translated by Ina Friedman and Haya Galai. New York: Oxford University Press, 1991.

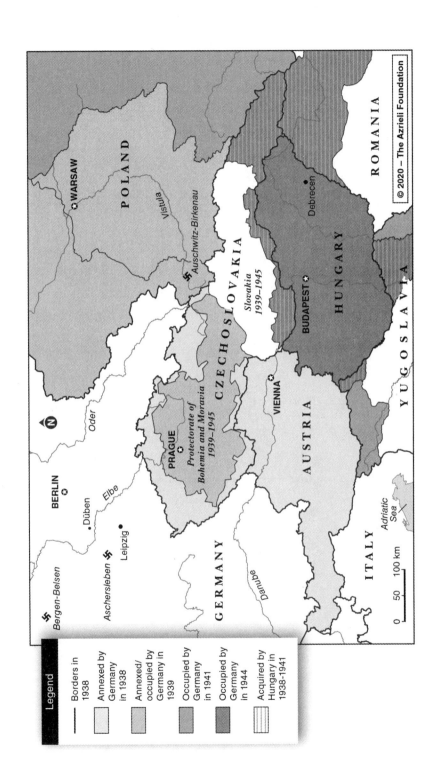

Legend

- Borders in 1938
- Annexed by Germany in 1938
- Annexed/occupied by Germany in 1939
- Occupied by Germany in 1941
- Occupied by Germany in 1944
- Acquired by Hungary in 1938-1941

POLAND

WARSAW

Vistula

Auschwitz-Birkenau

CZECHOSLOVAKIA

Slovakia 1939–1945

ROMANIA

© 2020 – The Azrieli Foundation

Debrecen

HUNGARY

BUDAPEST

PRAGUE

Protectorate of Bohemia and Moravia 1939–1945

VIENNA

AUSTRIA

YUGOSLAVIA

BERLIN

Düben

Elbe

Leipzig

Aschersleben

Oder

N

Bergen-Belsen

GERMANY

Danube

ITALY

Adriatic Sea

0   50   100 km

Judy Weissenberg Cohen Family Tree

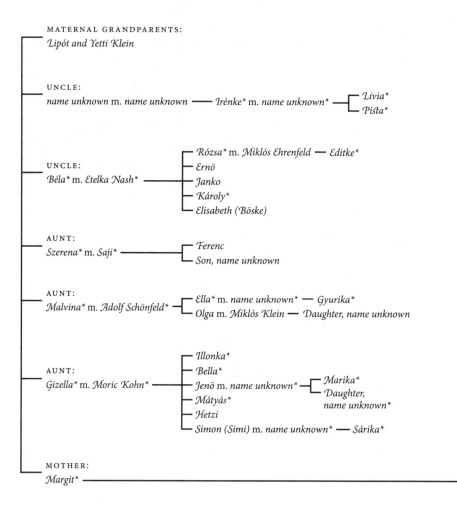

MATERNAL GRANDPARENTS:
Lipót and Yetti Klein

UNCLE:
name unknown m. *name unknown* ── *Irénke** m. *name unknown** ┌ *Livia**
└ *Pista**

UNCLE:
Béla* m. *Etelka Nash**
┌ *Rózsa** m. *Miklós Ehrenfeld* ── *Editke**
├ *Ernö*
├ *Janko*
├ *Károly**
└ *Elisabeth (Böske)*

AUNT:
Szerena* m. *Saji**
┌ *Ferenc*
└ *Son, name unknown*

AUNT:
Malvina* m. *Adolf Schönfeld**
┌ *Ella** m. *name unknown** ── *Gyurika**
└ *Olga* m. *Miklós Klein* ── *Daughter, name unknown*

AUNT:
Gizella* m. *Moric Kohn**
┌ *Illonka**
├ *Bella**
├ *Jenö* m. *name unknown** ┌ *Marika**
│   └ *Daughter,*
├ *Mátyás**   *name unknown**
├ *Hetzi*
└ *Simon (Simi)* m. *name unknown** ── *Sárika**

MOTHER:
Margit*

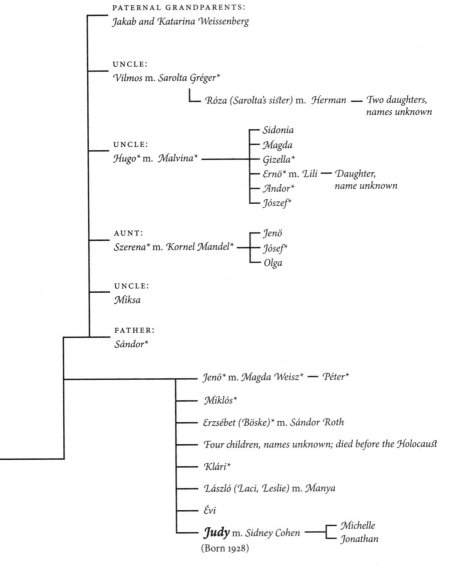

PATERNAL GRANDPARENTS:
Jakab and Katarina Weissenberg

UNCLE:
Vilmos m. *Sarolta Gréger**
        Róza (Sarolta's sister) m. *Herman* — *Two daughters, names unknown*

UNCLE:
*Hugo** m. *Malvina**
        Sidonia
        Magda
        *Gizella**
        *Ernö** m. *Lili* — *Daughter, name unknown*
        *Andor**
        *Jószef**

AUNT:
*Szerena** m. *Kornel Mandel**
        Jenö
        *Jósef**
        Olga

UNCLE:
Miksa

FATHER:
*Sándor**

*Jenö** m. *Magda Weisz** — *Péter**

*Miklós**

*Erzsébet (Böske)** m. *Sándor Roth*

Four children, names unknown; died before the Holocaust

*Klári**

László (Laci, Leslie) m. *Manya*

Évi

Judy m. *Sidney Cohen* — *Michelle / Jonathan*
(Born 1928)

*Murdered in
the Holocaust*

This memoir was written with infinite love and gratitude, in memory of my beloved sisters Böske, Klári and Évi, and my camp-sisters Sári and Edit Feig, without whose constant encouragement and help I would not have survived all the incredible hardships and atrocities we were subjected to in the camps. I would also like to honour the memory of my beloved parents, Margit and Sándor, and my brothers Leslie; Miklós; Jenö and his wife, Magda, and their infant son, Péter — as well as Uncle Vilmos and Aunt Sarolta, my surrogate grandparents.

The future historian will have to dedicate an appropriate page to the Jewish woman in the war. She will take up an important page in Jewish history for her courage and steadfastness. By her merit, thousands of families have managed to surmount the terror of the times.

Emanuel Ringelblum

Prologue

That year, 1944, everybody came: the believers, the atheists, the Orthodox, the agnostics — women of all descriptions and of every background. We were about seven hundred women, jammed into one long barracks. We were all there, remembering our homes and families on this Yom Kippur, the one holiday that had been observed in even the most assimilated homes.

We had asked for and received one candle and one *siddur* from the kapos. Someone lit the candle, and a hush fell over the barracks. I can still see the scene: the woman, sitting with the lit candle, starting to read Kol Nidre, the opening prayer of Yom Kippur.

The kapos gave us only ten minutes while they guarded the two entrances to the barracks to watch out for SS guards who might come around unexpectedly. Practising Judaism or celebrating any Jewish holiday was forbidden in the Auschwitz-Birkenau death camp. The Nazis knew it would give solace to the prisoners. But this particular year, some of the older women had asked two kapos for permission to do something for the eve of Yom Kippur.

Most of the kapos were brutalized and brutal people, but a few of them remained truly kind. We knew these particular two were approachable. One of the kind kapos was a tall blonde Polish woman, non-Jewish. The other one was a petite red-headed young Jewish woman from Slovakia.

When they had heard that we wanted to do something for Kol Nidre, the red-headed kapo was simply amazed that anyone still wanted to pray in that hellhole of Birkenau.

"You crazy Hungarian Jews," she exclaimed. "You still believe in this? You still want to do this, and *here*?"

Well, incredibly, we did — in this place where we felt that instead of asking for forgiveness from God, God should be asking for forgiveness from us. We all wanted to gather around the woman with the lit candle and *siddur*. She began to recite the Kol Nidre very slowly so that we could repeat the words if we wanted to. But we didn't. Instead, all the women burst out in a cry — in unison. Our prayer was the sound of this incredible cry of hundreds of women. I have never heard, before or since then, such a heart-rending sound. Something was happening to us. It was as if our hearts were bursting.

Even though no one really believed the prayer would change our situation, that God would suddenly intervene — we weren't that naive — the opportunity to cry out and remember together reminded us of our former lives, alleviating our utter misery even for the shortest while, in some inexplicable way. It seemed to give us comfort.

Even today, many decades later, every time I go to Kol Nidre services, I can't shake the memory of that sound. This is the Kol Nidre I always remember.

Treasured Years

Memories of my treasured childhood years in my hometown of Debrecen, Hungary, take me back to the time, too brief in my case, when my life was carefree and mostly happy.

I surmise I was unplanned, the seventh child in a family already crowded with three sons and three daughters. I was born on Monday, September 17, 1928. It was also the holiday of Rosh Hashanah, the Jewish New Year. My mother was thirty-eight years old when I was born, and as I was growing up she often seemed weary, except for her expressive, beautiful, large dark-brown eyes that could silently discipline us kids just by opening to a saucer-like size.

My mother, Margit Klein, was twenty years old when she married my father, Sándor Weissenberg (also spelled Weiszenberg), on Monday, June 6, 1910. During the next eighteen years, she had eleven births and one miscarriage. Four of her children died before the last four children were born, three of them tragically within one week in a city-wide scarlet fever and diphtheria epidemic. I was told by relatives that my mother became depressed and ill after this tragedy.

Most of my siblings were much older than I was. The three eldest were Jenö (1911); Miklós (1912); and Erzsébet, or Elizabeth, whom we called Böske (1916). Then there was an age gap because of the children who died. Then there was Klári (1922); László, or Laci (1924); and Évi (1925), who was the closest to me in age.

We lived in a Jewish area of the city, and our house at Nyugati utca 34 was one of three modest dwellings that centred around a courtyard. We had to open a huge iron door from the street to enter the property, and I can still visualize the long, heavy iron key, too large for me to use when I was a child. One of the dwellings belonged to my uncle Vilmos, my father's oldest brother, and his wife, Sarolta. Theirs was the largest house. In the third dwelling lived Sarolta's sister Aunt Róza with her husband, Uncle Herman, and their two grown daughters. We were a circle of extended family. All these dwellings were simple, as we were not rich, but the many potted plants in the courtyard, my mother's favourites, made it colourful and scented the air in the spring, summer and autumn. It was my job to water the plants as soon as I could reach them.

Beyond the courtyard there was a connecting doorway, a shortcut to my father's business, which was a large scrap iron and metal yard that also supplied small agricultural machinery. However, the official entry to the business was from the street, at Szepességi utca 39. My father sold every conceivable wrought iron and metal product, such as railway tracks and huge steel sheets, new and used; and the different scrap metals — bronze, brass, copper — and various items of the trade were stored in a number of covered sheds.

There were two other rooms where the business was. One was an office, and the other had been converted into a small prayer room that was equipped with a precious Torah scroll bought by Uncle Vilmos and Aunt Sarolta on one of their trips to Jerusalem. Jewish businessmen in our neighbourhood who didn't want to walk too far for daily prayers prayed in this small room twice a day with a *minyan*, which included my father, my uncle and at least eight other men.

Many years later, an archivist I had consulted about information on my family wrote a book about the history of Debrecen and included a chapter on the Jewish community. In it he mentioned that my father was a philanthropist. Every year my father donated money and materials to a trade school in Debrecen, contributing to the betterment of education in the city.

～

I remember being mischievous in my early childhood. I grew up in a very busy household full of siblings and constant activities of one kind or another, but little attention was paid to me. Some of the stories about my childhood I remember directly, others I remember because they were told over and over again.

There was the story of the wallet.

Once, when I was three or four years old, I asked my mother for a few pennies, Hungarian fillérs, because I wanted to go to the store to buy some candy. It was laundry day, and my mother was busy supervising the two hired washerwomen who came to do the washing for our large family. My mother dismissed me without giving me money. And so, when she wasn't looking, I lifted her wallet out of her apron pocket and took the fillérs myself. I didn't know what to do with the wallet once I had accomplished the theft, so I hid it under one of the huge cauldrons that was used to boil the white clothing and bedding. When it was time to pay the washerwomen, my mother couldn't find her wallet. Apparently, there was a big dispute, but I remained quiet. At night, after the fire under the cauldrons went down and Mari, our helper, cleaned out the ashes, she found the metal snap that had been on my mother's wallet. Somehow the evidence pointed toward me. And when I was asked, I admitted, amid tears, what I had done. Years later I asked my mother, "Did you punish me?" "No," she replied. "You were too young to understand the significance of what you did, burning all that money. We only scolded you."

Then there was the affair of the chicken.

One day I was entrusted to take a chicken to the *shoichet*, the religious slaughterer, to be killed. It was one of those tasks I loathed but had to do. We were having guests for dinner and the extra meat was needed. I was ashamed to be seen carrying the bird so I placed it in the bottom of a narrow satchel, just in case I met a friend. I arrived at the *shoichet* with a dead bird; the poor thing had suffocated. The *shoichet* would not touch it of course. It was a perfectly healthy chicken, but because it died a "natural" death before it could be slaughtered according to strict Jewish ritual, it was not kosher for us to eat. A woman who was working at the *shoichet*'s wanted the chicken's blood, for blood pudding I suppose, and cut its throat to drain it. But I had to go home with the dead bird and confess what had happened. To make matters worse, my punishment was to try to sell the chicken to one of our non-Jewish neighbours. I did manage to sell it at half the original price.

My rank in the family as the youngest had pros and cons. Our mother, whom we called Anyu, the Hungarian term for Mom, never indulged any of us as I recall. She had no time for that, and there was no favourite child or special time spent with any of us. Maybe that's why I was very precocious. I resented the fact that it wasn't only my parents who always told me what to do, but also my six siblings. Being the youngest was a double-edged sword, a burden and privilege. On the one hand, I was ordered around by my older siblings, and on the other hand, I was protected by my parents as the baby of the family.

Jenö, my oldest brother, who was seventeen years my senior, would address me by my nickname, "Jutka, go get me some cigarettes." Just like that! And I would reply, "You're not my father. You can't tell me what to do." I didn't like to be ordered around, period. I still don't. But if he paid me, I did it. What a mercenary!

Although we had a live-in maid because my mother was not well, the girls — never the boys! — all had to help with some housework. When there were tasks to be done, one of my siblings, usually Évi, would ask, "Where is Jutka? When is she going to do something to help around here?" Anyu would intervene, "Oh, leave her alone, she's just a child."

My sister Évi, who was three years older than I was, was my most frequent but rather reluctant babysitter. I vividly remember one incident when she grudgingly took me for a walk because Anyu had ordered her to. I don't know where she took me, but at one point she stopped and said, "Well, Jutka, this is the end of the world. I think I'm going to leave you here." I don't know how old I was, maybe four, but I got scared and started bawling. I was still bawling when we arrived home. Anyu asked why I was crying, and I told her, "Évi wanted to leave me at the end of the world." My sister was chastised for frightening me. But as much as she resented me then, we later became very close, and she took on a motherly role. We would often laugh heartily when recalling our childhood quarrels.

My father had a few siblings, but I remember only those who lived close by. There were Uncle Vilmos and Aunt Sarolta next door, who were childless and filled in like grandparents for us seven siblings. Uncle Vilmos had raised my father, who was seven years old when their father, Jakab, died, leaving their mother, Katarina, widowed. Portraits of my grandparents — dark, slightly frightening oil paintings — used to hang in our dining room, and as a young child I could not relate to them.

My father's brother Hugo had six children. He and Aunt Malvina lived on Szepességi utca, in a beautiful large home on the same street as our business. Uncle Hugo was quite rich I think and, according to my father, was a bit of a dandy. He loved to wear many gold rings and sported a small well-trimmed beard. He also had a much-admired automobile, a rarity in those days. We children felt ever so privileged to ride in it occasionally. I still remember the car windows, which were decorated with lovely short velvet curtains that had little gold pom-poms hanging at the edges. Father also had a sister, Szerena, and a brother Miksa.

When Hungary was carved up after World War I in the Treaty of Trianon, family ties were affected, especially in Anyu's family. She had a brother in what was now considered Slovakia, and his daughter, Irénke, and her children, Livia and Pista, would occasionally spend summer vacations with us. Livia was unforgettable to me with her flaming red hair, green eyes, freckled face and mischievous nature. Anyu's sister Szerena and her family lived in what was now Transylvania. We seldom saw them because we needed a visa to visit them.

Anyu's other brother, Béla, and two sisters, Giza and Malvina, lived in Debrecen and Biharnagybajom respectively, and my older siblings socialized a lot with their children, who were of the same age. There were many loud card games played in our home amid lots of laughter and joking. As a child I enjoyed just watching them, until the jokes got risqué and I was sent to bed.

We knew my maternal grandparents, Yetti and Lipót Klein, a little. They lived in the village of Biharnagybajom, and for many summers, Évi and I would spend a few weeks with them. It was an exciting visit because we travelled there by train. My grandparents owned the big general store on the main street, and I loved the various aromas in that store. I also strongly favoured a jar that sat on one of the counters. It held little square chocolates wrapped in paper with a picture of a cow, indicating that it was milk chocolate, and every so often we would receive a chocolate. Visiting there was a joy.

There is an incident from one of those visits that I don't know if I remember or if I just remember my parents talking about. One day I wandered off and didn't come home until late, and they were getting worried. Everyone in the village knew my grandparents, and they knew who I was, and finally somebody brought me home and told my grandparents, "Jutka ate something delicious in our home." "Yes, I ate the ear of a pig," I chimed in. The family had just killed a pig, and apparently I hadn't wanted to eat it because it wasn't kosher. But the family talked me into it, saying that it was okay because the ear was on the *outside* of the pig. I ate it and liked it. My grandparents laughed when they heard this, and of course I wasn't punished.

∿

I was five years old when Hitler came to power in Germany in 1933. Blissfully, I was unaware of the significance of this event and the kind of impact Hitler would have on my life, more than a thousand kilometres from Berlin.

Like most children, I happily attended kindergarten. I remember my first day well. As I timidly walked into the kindergarten room, Mrs. Almáshi, the teacher, suddenly called out, "Istenem! (Oh My God!) Here comes another Weissenberg." *How did she know?* I wondered. But of course she had recognized my coat, which had been worn by six Weissenbergs before me. It was a sheared mutton and had big pom-pom buttons with loops to fasten them, and could be worn by boys or girls. It seems it was an unforgettable coat.

I remember how on my second day of primary school, when Böske helped me put on my "new" six-times-handed-down leather school bag, she noticed how heavy it was. "Jutka, whatever did you put in this bag?" she asked. "Oh, just a few movie magazines to while away my boredom during recess," was my matter-of-fact reply. She burst out in good-natured laughter.

Böske was twelve years my senior and was like a surrogate mother to me. Whenever I had a problem or a pressing question, I would turn to her. With her kindness and infinite patience, mixed with a little teasing now and then, she answered my questions in ways I could understand. Then, one day after her wedding, in 1933, Böske disappeared from my life for several years. She married a fellow Hashomer Hatzair Zionist, Sándor Roth, in a seemingly genuinely joyous, all-night wedding celebration in our home. Most memorable was her dancing the hora and shredding the long, fine veil of her wedding dress as she did, to my utter dismay. I had secretly hoped to wear it one day.

Avid idealists, the newly wedded couple left for British Mandate Palestine, with Böske's enormous trousseau and all, to live on a kibbutz where they would help build a Jewish homeland, a move much opposed by my Orthodox father, who objected to the building of a secular Jewish nation. A while later my second-oldest brother, Miklós, would also leave for Palestine as a Hashomer *chalutz*, pioneer.

Then the letters came. Their secret contents were never revealed to us younger siblings, reflecting a common attitude toward children at that time, but my mother's tears when reading the letters indicated unhappiness all around. Selfish me! To *my* joy, and in an unforeseeably tragic move, Böske returned — minus her husband — in 1938, five years after she had left and amid grossly heightened anti-Jewish laws and sentiments in Hungary. My brother Miklós returned soon after. Later Böske would tell us more about her marriage and her life in Mandate Palestine, and about how disappointing her experiences with Zionism and kibbutz life were. The most shocking thing we would learn was that her marriage to Sándor was fake. My father wouldn't let Böske go to Palestine as a single woman, so she married a man who agreed that they would divorce as soon as they got to Palestine. However, once they were on the kibbutz, her new husband wanted to stay with her, and there was a dispute in the kibbutz over the whole situation. Böske eventually ended up moving to Tel Aviv and working as a governess for the rest of her time there.

~

The Jewish holidays were the highlight of our childhood years.

I just loved Purim, a festive holiday that celebrates the deliverance of the Jews from imminent doom at the hands of their enemies, a story told in the biblical Book of Esther, which my parents would hear read in the synagogue. For us kids the fun part was the endless baking, the heavenly aroma of cinnamon, cocoa and nutmeg wafting through the house, and the anticipation of eating my mother's delicious baked goods. I think Anyu was considered one of the best bakers among her friends. When Böske came back from Palestine, she took a course in making rich, sumptuous pastry. I can still see the heavily laden tables covered in mouth-watering pastries made by both of them. I especially remember Böske's *Rigó Jancsi*, a decadent chocolate mousse pastry. I still salivate just thinking about Purim.

Anyu was insistent about the tradition of giving *shalach manos*, gifts of food, and we children had the honour of delivering heavenly goodies to poor people as well as to friends and family. Our cousins who were our age would also come over on Purim, and we would play with our precious marbles. We didn't have fancy things, but we had a big yard and lots of space to play.

On Sukkot, the autumn harvest festival, the tradition is to build a hut called a *sukkah*, decorate it and eat meals in it for seven days. Our *sukkah* was unique because we used my uncle Vilmos's modern prefab *sukkah*. It was easy to put up, and only the dry vegetation, the *schach*, that covered the top of the *sukkah* was new every year. The *schach* was carefully arranged so that we could see the sky through the branches. My uncle had decorations for the interior of the *sukkah*, including his favourite, a picture of Emperor Franz Joseph wearing a hat. Hungarian Jews liked the emperor, who had been good to the Jews of the Austro-Hungarian Empire. Under his rule, in 1867 a bill passed emancipating the Hungarian Jews and giving them full equality as citizens. We would also decorate the *sukkah* by hanging walnuts, grapes and other fruits from the walls and *schach*. What we kids didn't like was eating in the *sukkah* on some of the colder evenings, as our ancestors might have done. But we were admonished for complaining, and indeed, we too weathered through it.

Passover, or Pesach, was a holiday that required a great deal of preparation. We cleaned the house from top to bottom to get rid of all *chametz* (bread and other leavened foods), and we replaced our ordinary dishes with dishes used only on Passover. It was quite an upheaval — like spring cleaning plus.

To this day, Passover conjures up bittersweet memories. There were many happy Passovers, and then there was the saddest of them all — the last one, in 1944, when my family, already partially decimated with our three brothers absent, was still together.

During the good times, at the Passover seder we usually had our immediate family plus Uncle Vilmos and Aunt Sarolta. After my brother Jenö got married, his wife, Magda, joined us too, so we had twelve or thirteen guests for both seder nights. Occasionally, we would have an unexpected guest as well.

The Passover story is about the ancient Hebrews' enslavement in Egypt and how they were freed, a story that is told in the biblical book of Exodus and is read at the seder from the Haggadah. To be truthful, as young children we didn't like reading the lengthy story of the Exodus. Our minds were mainly on "when is dinner?" but my father would read the Haggadah slowly, with *kavanah*, feeling. I would ask the Mah Nishtana, the Four Questions, because I was the youngest. Évi was very glad when I was old enough to recite the Four Questions and she was off the hook.

Évi was an odd character. She would have the Haggadah in front of her on the table, and underneath the table she would be reading a movie magazine, risking my father's wrath should he discover it. She was a gambler.

As we grew older, we learned to appreciate the Passover story, but we were still bored by the length of it and were ever so happy when dinner was served. The excellent wine we had was a good compensation though. A second cousin of my father's lived in the Tokaj wine region and owned a kosher winery. The area was noted for its excellent grapes that were made into world-famous, first-class wine. Every Passover this cousin sent us a gift of a small barrel of kosher wine, the only wine my father trusted to be kosher enough. The younger kids had small glasses, but one memorable Passover, Klári graduated to a regular wine glass and drank the mandatory four glasses of wine. She got good and drunk and started yelling, "My liver is on fire!" Off to bed she went!

After dinner we would sing one or two melodies, and then the kids would be put to bed while the men finished the Haggadah on their own.

For us children, the holiday of Chanukah meant watching our father light the *chanukiyah* in our window, one tiny wick for each of the eight nights of the holiday, and singing Chanukah songs. My mother made delicious *chremzli* patties, fried in oil, a Hungarian Jewish specialty, as a treat. Then we each received some pennies and started "gambling" with a *dreidl*, a spinning top that has different Hebrew letters on its four sides, which indicate if you win or lose when the *dreidl* stops spinning. That was lots of fun until our usual childish quarrels started.

Every Friday night my mother would light fourteen candles. I am not quite sure why fourteen. The set table always looked so festive with the white damask tablecloth, highly polished silver candlesticks, two large challahs covered with a cloth embroidered with the word "Shabbos," and the silver wine goblets for my father and brothers, who had each received one on their bar mitzvahs. When the fourteen candles were lit, I felt magic in the air. Anyu would wear a special white shawl instead of her usual kerchief and would make ingathering motions with her arms, welcoming the Shabbos. Then she would cover her eyes and say the prayer. With the onset of difficult times, Anyu started cutting the candles in half to save money; those fourteen flames still had to flicker. By then she often cried while saying the prayer. For me, the magic of it all dimmed irretrievably with our later sufferings. Today I can only guess what Anyu might have pleaded with her Almighty for.

My father was very strict about the Havdalah ceremony, which signified the end of Shabbos. I am not sure why, but it was important to him that we were all home for this ceremony. A beautiful, long multicoloured braided wax candle was lit and a prayer was said, and we had to smell some aromatic spices that were in a silver container. I wish my father had explained the meaning of any of it. Maybe his ritualistic Judaism would have had more influence on us if he had.

A Woman's Work

In the 1980s, my husband and I went to Hungary to visit some of my relatives who were still in Debrecen. We went out to eat at a Jewish restaurant, where we could have a real old-fashioned, tasty kosher meal. As we were sitting and eating, an elderly gentleman approached us and asked us who we were. I told him that I came from Canada now, but that I was originally from Debrecen. "My father's name was Sándor Weissenberg."

"I knew your parents," he said. "And I knew your mother even better than I knew your father." I got curious.

"In those days," he continued, "I was a yeshiva student who studied in Debrecen, but I came from a village. The custom was that Jewish families in Debrecen provided us out-of-town students with meals in their homes, and on the weekends we would go back home to our parents. For years, I ate at your mother's dining room table at least once a week, and sometimes twice a week. She was an outstanding lady. After I would finish my meal, she would prepare a food package for me. She would say, 'Here is a small snack for later,' but she would give me more than enough for a whole meal. And this happened every time I ate in your home. She was a kind and generous lady. I will never forget her."

His words brought tears to my eyes.

While my father contributed to society with his philanthropy, my mother contributed in other ways.

I remember my dear Anyu as a single-mindedly devoted mother to our large family. She was a tender, always busy, somewhat tired woman whom we dearly loved and respected but who seemed distant and perhaps weary of yet another chatterbox of a child like me in her menopausal years. Feeding a large family like ours, plus our live-in help, was more than a full-time occupation. It's difficult for me to imagine preparing three meals a day, every day, for ten people. But this was her life's work, and she was good at it.

The main meal was at noon. My father ate at exactly twelve o'clock every day. Then, after an hour-long nap, he would go back to the business until seven. All the siblings ate at various times after noon, depending on our school or work schedules. My tired mother would be serving us from noon to one-thirty. It was like a restaurant. Father liked quiet, peaceful mealtimes, but the interactions between us siblings were often noisy and filled with disputes, especially between my brother Laci and Évi, who were just one year apart. I can't imagine what the life of an only child would have been like.

Suppertime was after my father and my older brothers came home from the business, and it was usually a light meal. On winter evenings we had toasted rye bread rubbed with garlic and spread with chicken schmaltz, cold cuts and a lovely sweet tea. If we didn't have meat, we had a light dairy meal, but never the two together. We had a very kosher household.

Preparing food for winter was a major undertaking for my mother and Aunt Sarolta. All summer long they made fruit and vegetable preserves, jams and marmalade, pickles and tomato sauce, and many other delicacies, and we lived on all these goodies during the winter. This was a world in which ready-made food was not available or would have been shunned by proud homemakers like my mother. I love these memories of happy times, when mouth-watering aromas would permeate the air in our home.

I especially loved Anyu's preserves, like her red cherries in rum sauce. Oh, was that good! And then there were the walnuts — fresh and green and as big as plums — which we all had to help her prepare. First, every walnut had to be pierced twice with a fork, staining our hands with its juice. Then Anyu immersed them in a liquid sugar syrup and some alcohol. After three years, they would reach their ideal flavour and became the most delicious treat. I came to the conclusion at a young age that anything edible that was prepared with alcohol of any kind was bound to be delicious. I never lost the yen for these walnuts.

By the time I was ten years old, I often accompanied my mother when she went shopping for live poultry at the market where the farmers sold their livestock and produce. When I think back, I realize that her shopping skills were uncanny. She would pick up a hen and blow into its feathers to see the colour of its skin. And she would teach me. "See," she would say, "it is yellow. This is an old hen — good only for chicken soup." Or, when she was interested in buying a duck or goose, she would ask the farmer's wife, "Which village are you from, dear? Is there a creek near there? Do you let your birds wade in it?" If the answer was yes and yes, she would not buy the bird because of the likelihood that it had eaten fish while wading and would taste fishy.

Once she found the right birds, Anyu would get at least two and keep them in cages at home where they would be force-fed for a few weeks. When they were big and fat, they were slaughtered by the *shoichet*. The geese were then defeathered and cut into sections, cured in some kind of brine, and taken to the smokehouse to be smoked, which gave the meat flavour and longevity so that it would last through the winter. The meat was then hung in our cold pantry as we didn't have a refrigerator. We did have an icebox, but it was used mainly for milk and other dairy products. After the goose fat was rendered, it was put into large stone containers and used as the main cooking oil for meat dishes. The large goose livers were seared and served as a delicacy.

I can still see my mother and Aunt Sarolta working all summer just to have food for the winter. Anyu was proud of her cooking skills and kept some of the recipes a secret. She was devoted to her role as a homemaker and to looking after us. I don't know how she had the strength. She did have full-time live-in help, but it was still a lot of responsibility. It was her whole life, as it was for most of her female friends and neighbours. They were true unsung heroes!

It dawned on me years later how much being Orthodox and *shomeret* Shabbat, observant of the laws of Shabbos, was a blessing for Anyu. Her incredibly delicious cholent with the traditional kugel and a piece of smoked goose meat was prepared in advance and kept warm for Shabbos lunch in the ceramic oven after it was brought home from the bakery's oven, where it had cooked through the night. There was no cooking on Shabbos, and so she had a well-deserved rest. This was the day when she could put up her tired feet and avidly read the *Múlt és Jövő* (Past and Future), a Hungarian Jewish literary magazine — her favourite. This magazine closed down in 1944 but reopened for publication in 1988.

Our tightly knit Orthodox community was very charitable. I learned about *tzedakah*, charity, watching my mother. It was a religious obligation to help others, especially the poor, and to do *chesed*, acts of loving kindness. Anyu was involved with a circle of women who helped poor brides get everything they needed for their weddings and trousseaus. I was a curious onlooker at many of these women's meetings.

I also remember the dressmaker, who used to come to our home whenever we needed new dresses or coats, or when old ones had to be altered for the next sibling. We could not buy ready-made clothing in those days. The dressmaker was a religious woman with six children, and she would bring her baby with her. She was also the breadwinner in her household and always looked tired, with watery red eyes and puffed eyelids. When I asked Anyu why this woman was working so hard, she answered that it was because her husband was a Torah scholar and was sitting in the synagogue all day and studying.

All day? I wondered. *Couldn't he help her just a bit?* But I was afraid to ask.

Occasionally there were family disputes about money. I think my parents were financially comfortable, and yet, with that many children, especially with all those tuition fees, funds were limited. Often, when we went shopping downtown, my mother would remark, "You see that big corner apartment building? It could have been ours if your father had listened to me."

What was the big dispute?

"During World War I," she explained, "I told your father, 'Sándor, we have some extra money. We don't know how the war will end. Let's put half of that money in dollars and only half in German marks.' That was *my* opinion. Father didn't listen to me; he did what *he* decided to do. He put everything in marks. With Germany and Austria-Hungary losing the war, the German marks became worthless."

We also knew that my mother managed the business while looking after two children when my father was called up to serve in World War I. Reportedly, she was very good at that too. It's amazing how much talent the women I knew had. However, they didn't always have a chance to prove it.

Ominous Times

There were probably days when I was angry at my older brothers or sisters or when I was denied things I badly wanted, but all in all, I recall my childhood as mostly pleasant. The fear began when I was ten years old.

In 1936, when I was eight, Nazi Germany began to expand, starting with the occupation of the Rhineland. This was also when large-scale institutionalized discrimination against Jews in Germany began. In March 1938, Germany annexed Austria in an event known as the Anschluss, and then took over the Sudetenland area of Czechoslovakia. In the same year, in November, there were the violent pogroms of Kristallnacht and the two-day wholesale destruction of more than two hundred synagogues and Jewish properties in Germany and Austria. Approximately thirty thousand German Jews were sent to concentration camps.

As all this took place next door to us in Austria and Czechoslovakia, we were frightened by what the prospects were for us Jews in Hungary. Only a young child at the time, it was scary for me to hear how worried my parents were by this news. Then Germany went on to take over the rest of Czechoslovakia in March 1939, and no one stopped them, and my parents agonized even more.

During this time, many Austrian and Czech Jews were fleeing to Hungary, and every so often there were mass arrests of Jewish refugees. Decent members of the Debrecen police force would warn my father when this was going to happen so that he could inform others in the Jewish community. Some of the sheds our family business used for scrap metal had small attics, and over the next two years we would hide people in these narrow spaces until the roundups were over. Some people had to hide for several days. At one time there were seventeen people hidden in our attics. My father was a righteous person.

When World War II broke out on September 1, 1939, there was still relative tranquility in Hungary, but political and societal attitudes were changing in frightening ways. Arrow Cross (Nyilas) fascist thugs appeared on our streets. Tens of thousands of Jews were dismissed from their jobs, losing their livelihoods, which made life increasingly difficult. The government was becoming more right wing and introduced a number of anti-Jewish laws and edicts between 1938 and 1941 to appease radical antisemitic groups, aligning themselves with the Nazis, who were becoming more and more influential in Hungary. One anti-Jewish law restricting what kinds of businesses Jews could engage in required my father to close down his business in 1940. None of the authorities cared how a family of nine would manage without an income.

As these changes were happening, daily life remained relatively normal, and I continued going to school. All my schooling took place in Jewish parochial schools, and I had only Jewish friends right through my school years, except for the non-Jewish neighbourhood children I played with. In Grade 1, we had started learning two languages, Hebrew and German. I participated in school plays I really enjoyed, and once I even sang a solo. There were four years of elementary school and two years of middle school, *polgári*. During my time in *polgári*, I would attend a service for students in the beautiful synagogue on Deák Ferenc utca on Saturday mornings. The Orthodox synagogue didn't have such activities for girls, but my religious father was just glad that I was attending Jewish activities. Services there were conducted by the young rabbi of Debrecen, Pál (Meir)

Weisz, and some older students. The girls would sit upstairs in the women's balcony, and the boys were downstairs. Oh, the melodies! The singing of the prayers stays with me till today. The music alone felt like a prayer. Those were the days when I still believed in prayer.

After the services were through, all the students would go for a leisurely walk on the grounds of the Déri Museum, where there were beautiful gardens. This is where we tried to flirt with the boys and vice versa. The boys would walk in one direction, and the girls would walk in the opposite direction so that we could "accidentally" meet. That was the real fun.

By the time I reached high school age at fifteen, most Jewish students in Hungary were not allowed to enter the local Catholic or Protestant high schools anymore. My sister Klári had attended a Catholic high school that had a very high academic standard and was able to finish her last year there in spite of the decrees. Évi went to a commercial high school where she learned dressmaking along with academic subjects. But I was no longer allowed to go to a local school, and there was no Jewish high school for girls in Debrecen, which was typical of Orthodox communities in that era. The Jewish leadership had no choice but to make the boys' high school a co-educational one. So that's where I went to school for one unfinished year.

My father's business had already been closed down for a few years at this point, and our savings were low. The government had stopped supporting Jewish high schools, and the Jewish community was not rich enough to provide free tuition. My father told me that if I paid half my tuition fee, he would pay the other half. So I found a job tutoring middle-school children and would go to their homes after school to help them with their school work.

My high school classroom was a crowded one with sixty students, but the ratio of girls to boys was great: fifteen to forty-five. Needless to say, the girls were very popular, but during recess we were separated from the boys. Heaven forbid we should mingle with boys during school hours! Still, we had unexpected, youthful fun.

While I was experiencing the dramas and joys of youth, dark clouds were gathering. In November 1940, the Hungarian government had entered the Axis alliance, and Hungary became not only an ideological but also a political and military ally with Nazi Germany. Many Jewish men were forced into labour battalions, and so, while we still attended school, and maybe had some fun too, our Jewish community was deprived of almost all its husbands, fathers, brothers and sons — all able-bodied men, who were drafted and taken away.

Fifty thousand Jewish forced labourers were sent to the Eastern Front, into Soviet Ukraine with the Hungarian Second Army in 1942, and fewer than ten thousand would return. The Jewish servicemen were assigned the most dangerous work, such as clearing minefields ahead of the advancing army, and they were often treated cruelly by their Hungarian officers and guards, especially during the Hungarian army's retreat in the winter of 1943.

I think the words of the Hungarian memoirist György Beifeld in his 1943 diary portray something of the experience my brothers, cousins and thousands of other Hungarian Jewish men must have had:

The wind was blowing icicles into our eyes. Our breath got frozen to the fabric we used to cover our faces. One's legs were in great pain dragging the body... Anyone who got exhausted and sat down for a minute would inevitably freeze to death. That applied equally to men and horses. They lay there next to each other frozen to death, a soldier, a horse, and a Jew.[1]

From the time the men were taken from Debrecen, I recall some old men, but mainly women and girls, shouldering all the daily tasks,

---

1   "Art and Survival: György Beifeld's Visual Memoir from the Russian Front, 1942–1943." United States Holocaust Memorial Museum. Accessed 2018. https://encyclopedia.ushmm.org/content/en/article/art-and-survival-gyoergy-beifelds-visual-memoir-from-the-russian-front-1942-1943.

caring for the children, running businesses, earning a living in cottage industries, attending to the sick and poor in the community.

In my home, it was mainly my mother and Böske who took care of the family and business, facing heartbreaking worries coupled with real physical hardships. My poor father, no longer able to provide for his family, became demoralized; his cherished sons Jenö and Miklós had been sent far away, exposed to deadly dangers, as the scarce reports informed us. But Böske was there like the Rock of Gibraltar. She had returned from Palestine as a politically mature, seasoned Hashomer Hatzair socialist and understood a lot more about the political situation in Europe than the others in my family. My father, in denial about the political realities, relied more and more on her, sometimes begging, "Bring me some good news, even if it is a lie."

Böske also returned from Palestine with a good grasp of English and Hebrew. And so she became a private English teacher to many students and made a handsome living. She also attempted to teach us younger siblings, tirelessly trying to convince us how important it was to know a language besides Hungarian ("useless beyond Hungary's borders," she often said), but we didn't take her seriously — to our regret many years later. But who knew that then?

I think it was in 1942 or 1943 when my mother encouraged Böske to escape Hungary by applying for domestic positions in Britain. Because she spoke English well, she had a good chance of being hired as cheap labour in the United Kingdom. Her passport and photo were ready, and there was even an employer waiting for her, when the borders were closed and the opportunity to be free was lost.

Évi, who was very bright but not scholastically inclined, had golden fingers, and after high school, she apprenticed in an haute couture dress salon at my mother's insistence. Idle hands were not permitted in our home. Évi was talented and had a creative mind, and she learned to sew with a messianic zeal that became a blessed survival tool; in some ways, sewing saved her life. Évi was just like my mother in so many respects; I never saw either of them idle.

In 1944, Klári, twenty-two years old, beautiful and vivacious but prone to melancholy, was the victim of anti-Jewish policies that had started in 1920 as the *numerus clausus* law, which were followed in 1938 by more restrictive laws excluding Jewish students from universities. Laci was affected by these policies as well, and so they took the only option that was left and started working. Laci worked as an electrician's apprentice and Klári as a bookkeeper in the import/export business of her best friend Elizabeth Neumann's father. However, she was very anxious to leave because of the rumoured fate of beautiful girls being sexually abused in Nazi-occupied European countries and by soldiers on the front. There was a rumour that somebody met a young woman in Budapest whose arm was tattooed with "Nur für Deutsche Soldaten" (only for German soldiers). In my post-retirement years, as I did research on the conditions of women during the Holocaust, I discovered that there were brothels established for German soldiers on the front and in some concentration camps as an incentive for the slave labourers to be more productive.

Klári badly wanted to go to Budapest where she thought that she could melt into a larger non-Jewish society and it would be safer for her. She had a plan to study nursing under the tutelage of a cousin. My father sabotaged that plan because of his rigid religious principles, but Klári was still determined to leave. She managed to obtain "Aryan" identity papers from a friend from her Catholic high school, and she left town to hide in full view as a Christian in Budapest, where she hoped no one would recognize her.

~

It was during my one unfinished year of high school, in 1943–1944, that the political situation became more unpredictable. These were worrisome, turbulent times, and it was difficult for us to concentrate on our studies. Those who had transistor radios turned them on to listen to the news, including our teachers. We also learned the frightening news from the Slovakian-Jewish refugees entering Hungary, including our own relatives, Irénke, Livia and Pista, the cousins from Eperjes, Hungary, which was now Prešov, Slovakia, who used to visit us long ago, on those good old peaceful summer days. Now, Livia's red hair had to be dyed black so that our Christian neighbours wouldn't recognize her and betray her to the authorities. They too found refuge in the attics of our scrap metal sheds.

This was a time when we, the young, were worried, and yet we were still teenagers and wanted to have fun. Some of us — Agi Loson-czi and her sister Anna, Zsuzsi Kalmancy and her brother Peter, plus a few others — went on picnics in Nagyerdő, the Grand Forest, just outside of Debrecen, enjoying ice cream and lots of laughter. We were very alive and very foolish with our pretense of normalcy. Yet, we had to grow up fast too. At home we constantly heard the adults' hushed, worried conversations. We were all sworn to strict secrecy about our German Telefunken shortwave radio, which was hidden in the cellar. We would listen to the British Broadcasting Corporation's Hungarian news report daily, wanting to hear news from a real source — not from the Hungarian state radio broadcast, which just made pronouncements of victories. Later on, when things were much worse, I would hear the echo of my mother's often repeated plea, "Gott im Himmel (God in Heaven), what next?" — the unanswered question to her Almighty: "What else will we have to endure?"

For some reason, we continued to have naive hope that the war would end soon and we Jews in Hungary would escape the horrors the rest of Europe was experiencing. But our hopes were soon dashed. Not a word was said about the concentration or death camps, even though we now know that the Allied governments to some extent knew about them by then.[2]

---

2 See *Human Rights after Hitler: The Lost History of Prosecuting Axis War Crimes*,
   by Dan Plesch, who demonstrates that United Nations documents that were
   unsealed in 2017 indicate that Soviet, UK and US governments were aware of the
   mass murder of Jews as early as December 1942. More information about this
   unsealed archive is available at www.unwcc.org.

Changed Forever

Our lives immediately and profoundly changed on March 19, 1944. When the Nazis became aware that Hungary wanted to withdraw from the Axis alliance and that Miklós Horthy was making overtures to the Allies, the German army marched into Hungary and occupied it, with SS officer Adolf Eichmann in charge of ghettoizing and deporting the Jews.

Matters proceeded with lightning speed. Shortly after the German occupation, all Jewish schools had to close their doors. My memories of that time are of constantly worried faces and whispered discussions among the adults around us. The children absorbed their grave concerns by osmosis, and our childhoods were not allowed to blossom as we lived with uncertainty from day to day.

The brutal events that followed in rapid succession happened with the full cooperation and participation of the newly installed pro-German prime minister, Döme Sztójay, along with the bureaucrats, the police, the dreaded, brutal gendarmes, and the "good" people who were waiting with jaundiced eyes to loot our homes.

On March 31, Jews were ordered to wear a yellow Star of David, cut from canary yellow cloth and in a specified size; it had to be worn on an outer garment when we were in public. We became a visible minority, and life became precarious. I remember riding on the streetcar to visit the students I tutored. The yellow star was attached to my jacket as it legally had to be, but I covered it with the books and notes I was holding. This was my little act of resistance. At one point my father was called into the Gestapo headquarters to face demands for gold that we didn't have. He was tortured by having the soles of his feet badly beaten, and he walked home in great pain.

My father's barber of some thirty years offered to hide us all until the end of the war since the Soviets were already very close, but my naive father said no: "What happens to all of us Jews here will happen to me too." End of argument — he was the sole decision maker. Actually, the barber would have had to hide us for less than a year, until the area was liberated by the Soviet army on October 19, 1944. But by then, most Hungarian Jews who were deported from the provinces had been murdered in Auschwitz-Birkenau. The eastern part of Hungary was Judenfrei, free of Jews.

Additional restrictions and edicts were rapidly introduced, and on May 9, the Debrecen ghetto was established in the area of the city where most of the Jews lived. The ghetto was divided in two by a street — a "large" and "small" ghetto — allowing the non-Jewish population to carry on with their daily activities unhindered. Non-Jews had to leave the area where the ghetto was to make room for the Jews who were transferred in. The ghetto was cordoned off behind temporary wooden walls. Large numbers of our extended family moved into our home, which was inside the ghetto boundaries, and there seemed to be people everywhere. It was terribly overcrowded, especially at night when we all had to lie down to sleep — it was wall-to-wall people. Of course, the toilet facilities became hopelessly inadequate. We were allowed two hours a day to do grocery shopping. However, that was in the late afternoon, when the stores were mostly empty of goods. Our isolation from our neighbours and the rest of the population of Debrecen was now complete.

Young as I was, I sensed misery all around me. The women tried to make meals with the meagre supplies they could get, but it was never enough. I worked as a volunteer nurse's helper in the makeshift hospital that was housed in what had been the Jewish high school. Teenagers were often given the task of playing with younger children, who were very restless or upset with the upheaval around them, especially when there was an Allied bombing. But our ghetto life didn't last long enough for us to organize anything meaningful for the little ones. Lack of adequate food and medical supplies, lack of freedom and lack of privacy made life seem more and more hopeless every day.

My parents asked me to correspond with my youngest brother, Laci, who was stationed in Hungary as a forced labourer. In one of my letters, I poured out my complaints about everything that we were lacking in the ghetto, but above all I bemoaned our loss of freedom. After the war, when I met up with Laci, I found out that the correspondence was checked and that Laci was punished for my complaints and had to do about forty push-ups. Deranged fascist logic!

There was one bright spot, a ray of light that shone through the dark clouds in the form of some unexpected clandestine help. There was a set of windows in our home that opened onto Nyugati utca, which was one of the boundaries of the ghetto. The authorities had boarded the windows from the outside so that we could not make contact with the outside world. But one night we heard a faint knocking on one of the boards. Voices from outside told us that they were friends and that they had food for us. The board was removed, food was quickly handed through the window and the board was replaced. After the war I did some research about Christian groups in Debrecen who were active in the resistance, and I surmised that these kind people were most likely Seventh-day Adventists. Whatever faith they belonged to, they dared to follow their own ethical compass and refused to be bullied into indifference or hatred. They represented one tiny bright light in the prevailing societal darkness. They repeated their noble deed once more.

From the ghetto, Father sent a farewell letter to Klári in Budapest, a fatal mistake. Klári came back to say her last goodbye to the family and stayed too long. The ghetto was closed and escape was impossible. Klári was trapped and became depressed. Her spirit returned once for a few brief seconds when a Hungarian policeman came to our home to order us to gather for deportation. He noticed her nice little wristwatch, a high school graduation gift from our parents, which she had refused to hand in to the authorities. The Hungarian police officer, while polite enough, demanded it. Klári very slowly took it off, and then smashed it against the wall. With a smirk on her face, she looked into the man's eyes and said, "*Now* you can have it." Surprisingly, nothing happened to her. The policeman must have known what her fate would be very shortly.

Our time in the ghetto did not last very long. Six memorable and miserable weeks altogether. Little did we know then how well off we were in comparison with what was to come.

On June 21, 1944, the ghetto was emptied, and we were transferred to the nearby Serly brickyards. I can still picture our march through the city to the brick factory, many of our neighbours lining the sidewalks, watching and laughing (there was the odd tear). These people, many of whom had been friendly with our parents for thirty some years, had become adversaries in a mere couple of years, some in a few months. It was difficult for my young mind to understand this, and it is still incomprehensible. As we learned after the war, many of these neighbours could hardly wait for us to be deported, and as soon as we were, they looted our homes, grabbing those few wretched items the Nazi occupiers hadn't confiscated.

We were housed in this factory, which was unfit for humans to live in, for about eight days. We hung up blankets to create tiny private spaces, especially for our parents and for elderly and religious people. Recently dug ditches with some wooden planks thrown across served as latrines. There was no separation for males and females. This was a most humiliating and degrading experience for all of us; the shame felt by everyone was palpable.

Then came the lineup and waiting for the cattle cars. Ironically, when they came, we felt relief.

~

Thursday, June 29, 1944. The deportation began with Hungarian soldiers pushing and shoving people into the cattle cars. It is impossible to adequately describe this bewildering development — the physical, emotional and psychological turmoil experienced inside the car, overflowing with seventy-eight people. The elderly sat on the floor, a few on the bedding or small suitcases they brought along. The mothers with infants or toddlers tried to find space. The young people, like my sisters and I, stood, packed like herring in a jar and perspiring profusely in the heat. We were provided with two pails, one with drinking water and an empty one to use as a toilet. Of course, there was no privacy. It didn't take long for the crying and children's whining to blend horribly with the stench emanating from the makeshift open toilet. My father, a pious Jew, prayed a lot, but judging from the expression on his face, I am certain he felt betrayed by his God. My mother cried quietly. My eighteen-month-old nephew, Jenö's son, Péter, who was sick, whined constantly for food we didn't have, and all seventy-eight of us thirsted for water that was in short supply.

Indeed, the dreadful atmosphere in the cattle car foreshadowed something ominous to come. The rich family life and community I chronicled so lovingly earlier had been left behind and was now only a treasured memory. Gone were those happy, carefree school years with my youthful trials and tribulations. In the cattle car they all seemed utterly trivial.

A Place Beyond Imagining

We arrived at the end of the journey on July 3, tired, parched and bewildered, in an indescribable place: barbed wire, electrified fences and SS soldiers with their trained dogs waiting on the platform — all of them, man and beast, barking constantly. Our arrival, early in the morning, in Auschwitz-Birkenau, is an infinitely agonizing memory of an astonishing and traumatic new experience. Arriving in this nightmarish place was shocking and disorienting, beyond anything we ever saw or could have imagined. One heart-stopping event followed another.

Two male prisoners dressed in striped pyjama-like uniforms opened the heavy sliding doors of the cattle cars and jumped in. We welcomed the whiff of fresh air that trickled in. One of the men immediately started yelling, "Heraus! Heraus!" (Out! Out!) at the top of his lungs, but the other one whispered to the women who were holding babies or little children's hands, telling them in a hushed, urgent tone, "Give the children to the grandmothers." He repeated this many times without any explanation. From what I observed, few if any women heeded his urging. I never forgot this scene.

It was decades after the war that a very fine scholar and daughter of Hungarian Jewish survivors, Gail Ivy Berlin, did research on the Kanada *Kommando*, the group of male prisoners responsible for emptying the cattle cars and sorting the new transports' belongings.

These workers knew that the grandmothers and the children would be murdered right away, but that young women without children were not sent to die immediately. And so they warned the young mothers to hand over the children to grandmothers, initiating a form of resistance not formally recognized in Holocaust history.[1]

After disembarking, men and women were immediately separated. This was the last time I saw my father, who was sixty years old. A high-ranking SS medical officer (we learned later on that this might have been the infamous Dr. Josef Mengele) then selected us, the women, by moving his thumbs only — left or right. Mothers with children, visibly pregnant women and all the elderly were sent to the left. My sister-in-law, who was holding her infant son, kept holding him. Being a father didn't automatically sentence a man to death in Birkenau, but being a mother, or just holding the little hand of a child, even if the child wasn't your own, meant instant death in the gas chambers. Young women like me and my three sisters, who seemed fit enough for work, were sent to the right. We didn't know what either direction meant, that we were actually being sentenced.

This was when I saw my mother for the last time, walking arm in arm with Aunt Sarolta, her lifelong best friend. We had to part in an instant, without a goodbye or a hug — which I still miss at my advanced age of ninety-one.

And yet, I was lucky, for I had my three older sisters with me. At least for a little while we were sentenced to live and could stay together. But who could ever be prepared for the unthinkable and the unimaginable we were to face?

Shortly after the first and fatal selection, we were taken to an ugly grey building the Nazis deceptively called "the sauna." There we were

---

1   Berlin's full article about the Kanada *Kommando* can be accessed on Judy Cohen's website, "Women and the Holocaust — a Cyberspace of Their Own," at http://www.theverylongview.com/WATH/.

ordered to undress — to the nude. They stripped us of our clothing, then shaved off all the hair on our bodies. Naturally, we felt humiliated and degraded, being forced to stand naked in front of all those SS men, the female guards and their prisoner underlings. We were disinfected with an awful-smelling liquid that burned our freshly shaven areas. Our feminine sensitivities were callously trampled on. For years after the war I would not use bleach; it had a distinct Birkenau odour.

Then we were allowed to have a two-minute cold shower, and we desperately drank the shower water because we were parched from our journey in the cattle cars. We were then sent outside, wet as we were, no towels. Luckily it was July and hot, and we dried quickly in the sun.

A female kapo, who we learned was also a prisoner but with some authority, gave us something to cover our naked bodies with. There was a huge pile of used clothing, disinfected from lice but otherwise mostly dirty, from which the kapo would randomly pick a "garment" and throw it to us. It did not matter if it fit, and if we complained we were beaten.

I received a very long, light blue nightgown with a pretty flower pattern; it was much too long for me to walk in. I looked around, wondering fearfully where my sisters were. And yet they were all around me, looking like weird strangers. Only their voices were familiar. In spite of our utter misery, we burst out laughing. Bald and dressed in dirty rags, we were quite a tragicomic sight!

Böske, always the practical one, tore a large segment of material from the bottom of my nightgown, just below the knee. She tore the cloth into four long narrow scarves to cover, in turban fashion, our bald heads. Instant magic! We felt less humiliated and just a tiny bit feminine again. The cloth also protected our freshly shaved scalps from the searing sun.

After this ordeal, we were marched to the section of the camp that would become our home for a few months, BIII or "Mexico." It had been quickly constructed to hold some of the almost half a million Hungarian Jews who were deported in a short amount of time, but the construction was not completed. It was the least equipped camp in Birkenau. Many of the barracks were completely empty, with no bunk beds. With hundreds of women in each barracks, we slept on the bare wooden floors, tightly packed in. If one person wanted to turn over, the whole row had to turn as well. Évi, Klári, Böske and I cried through that first night, along with all the others. I think the next time we cried wasn't until our tightly knit foursome was broken up.

The day started early in the morning when it was still chilly outdoors, but we all had to go to roll call, *Zählappell*, regardless of the weather. Roll call was a torture in itself. If one prisoner was missing from the count, we stood there, rain or shine, until the person was found — usually dead. Another roll call was conducted in the evening. After the morning roll call, we would receive a hot brown liquid that hardly resembled coffee.

One incident remains etched in my mind. On this particular day, Irma Grese, the well-known sadist and brutal *Aufseherin*, senior female overseer, came to inspect the roll call. One feeble prisoner, a young girl, was about four seconds late. Irma Grese, only twenty years old at the time, pointed her out, and with a crooked forefinger indicated to her to come forward and stand near her. Trembling, the girl obeyed. Irma started to kick her with the highly polished black leather boots she always wore. She kicked and kicked the girl mercilessly until that poor soul expired right under her feet while hundreds of us looked on, frozen and impotent with fear and numbed by extreme disgust. It did my revengeful soul a great deal of good when I learned after the war that this monster was captured in Bergen-Belsen and was tried and executed by a British military court in December 1945, along with a few others of her ilk. Or, considering her dastardly acts, was a quick death too kind for her?

During these dreaded, twice-daily roll calls, I was always the second or third in a row of five so that my sisters could shield me from the cold, the heat or the wind. I can't remember who our designated fifth was from day to day but eventually she too became family.

There was no running water or proper toilet facilities in BIII, not even a latrine. Certain corner areas were cordoned off and equipped with a pail. That was it. I can't recall what we used for toilet paper. A water truck brought us drinking water once a day, and there was near rioting to be able to obtain a cupful of water, as we were all parched from the constant heat. Since we didn't have running water in "Mexico," we were taken to another camp for a shower once a week. During one of those walks to the other camp, as we passed some lumber being piled high by male prisoners, I heard someone yell, "Juszuf!" which had been my nickname in high school, back in Debrecen.

I looked up, and sure enough, it was one of my former classmates who, astonishingly, recognized me, in rags, head shaved! How had he recognized me? He called out to me, "On the way back, look up. I'll have something for you." Indeed, on the way back, he threw down a small package. In it was a small piece of real rose-scented soap, two sewing needles and some thread — real treasures in that depraved world we were in. Évi's talented hands made very good use of the needles, mending our torn clothes. The piece of soap, which I shared with my sisters, rekindled some very pleasant memories. I worried though; we never saw my classmate again. I hoped no SS overseer had noticed what he did for me and punished him for it.

Böske was preoccupied with our survival, keenly aware of what was going on around us. She understood clearly that in Birkenau murder was taking place on a large scale. Among the first things she did was borrow a knife and get hold of a piece of wood from which she made four spoons. With these spoons she literally force-fed us younger siblings by instructing us to hold our noses and swallow the awful smelling, looking and tasting *Dörrgemüse* soup, a liquid made from dried vegetables that was dished up to us as something edible. We often found bugs, little stones, broken pieces of glass and grass in it, besides the ever-present turnip. Someone suggested that the

Nazis had mowed the grass somewhere and that all the cuttings were thrown into hot water and that's what was served to us. I can still hear Böske's voice: "We must survive. Eat, eat, please, eat!"

At noon, prisoners delivered the food in large, heavy cauldrons to a central area. Böske managed to become one of the people delivering the food, which meant that she received an extra piece of bread. At first, we didn't want to eat the *Dörrgemüse*, but eventually we became so hungry that we ate anything. Initially, we had one bowl that we shared among five people: my sisters, me and another person who also became like family. The first person in our lineup would get the bowl filled and then everybody would take a sip. Later on, each of us received our own bowl. Usually, people would rush to get the food. But we realized that the thicker part was at the bottom, so it was wise to wait. There were often scuffles around who would get the thick bottom food.

For supper we received a loaf of bread for five people, and someone would divide the bread into five equal pieces. Everyone watched to make sure the portions were even, that no one would get a millimetre more or less than anyone else. We also received one slice of salami or a small piece of cheese, usually a type called kvargli, or margarine. Hunger drove a lot of people to steal. There were stories of mothers stealing from daughters and vice versa. If you didn't finish your bread right away, you had to hide it under your head at night or somewhere else safe to protect it from thieves. Self-preservation came first in Birkenau.

As the days went by, we became aware of a strange stench permeating the air, day and night. We did wonder where those who had been sent to the left at our arrival were: our parents; Jenö's wife, Magda, with their infant son, Péter; cousins with their young children. We were told we would see them later — lies, all shameful, unadulterated lies! I am not sure exactly how the knowledge reached us that those sent to the left were murdered in the gas chambers, right away or overnight, their bodies burned in the adjacent crematoria. Many bodies were also burned in open pyres when the Hungarian Jewish transports came, often one after another, as the crematoria were overloaded. *That* was the strange stench in our nostrils day and night — the burning flesh of our beloved family members.

Even though we lived with that knowledge, our hearts broken, there was no time or opportunity to mourn. Every ounce of our being was needed for survival and survival alone. Mourning came much later.

Our existence in Birkenau, this most devastating place on earth, a place beyond all imagining, was precarious. Loud screaming by the Lager leaders of "Achtung! Achtung!" (Attention! Attention!) always sent shivers down our spines and inevitably meant selections, the most gut-wrenching times, worse even than hunger. We had to file in front of a camp physician, possibly the "Angel of Death" himself, Mengele, usually naked, for inspection. Those who were considered too skinny or who showed signs of illness or had a rash were sent to their deaths by gas. The fear in anticipating these events engulfed me at all times. We never knew what would happen at a selection, which of us would be sent to work somewhere in Germany or to another camp or to be gassed. My biggest challenge was overcoming a fear of remaining alone. My stomach was always in a knot, bowels ready to burst because I felt safe only near my sisters. Eventually I developed a stomach ulcer.

There we were, facing moral tests and threats to our existence daily, but I cannot recall us four sisters ever fighting about anything. Mostly we worried. Our concern for each other withstood the most appalling and challenging conditions. Looking back, I see how each of us sisters endured every degrading and humiliating treatment in Birkenau while supporting each other, and also with the skills, dispositions and apprehensions each of us came with.

Böske proved to be a pillar of strength, always compassionate with a helping hand or word, just like at home — the most decent human being I ever knew and one whom I loved and admired. She was and is my greatest role model.

Klári was very fragile, like a delicate flower, and from the very beginning, without a smile. She was now in the place she feared most and had wanted to avoid at all costs, and almost did, if it had not been for my father's insensitivity to her fears. Her melancholy would deepen with each passing day, though she expressed little emotion one way or another.

Évi, easy-going and phlegmatic as always, found school friends from way back when and chatted away her hunger as much as she could, or repaired torn clothes with the needles my classmate gave us. She also had a very pleasant singing voice and sang from time to time with some of her friends, to everyone's sheer delight.

Most of the women in the camp stopped menstruating pretty soon after our arrival. In a way we were glad, from a sanitary point of view. Some believed that the Nazis had put something in our food or drink to stop our menstrual flow. Others thought we stopped menstruating because our bodies were in shock. I remember reading an early memoir in which the survivor surmised that this was one of "Hitler's rewards" — for Jewish women not to be able to have children, even if they did survive. Fortunately, this was not the case.

Every day we witnessed people dying. Some died from hunger, some from disease, some from exhaustion. During the never-ending roll calls, some of the weaker girls would collapse and die, right there and then. I saw young girls who could potentially be my classmates dropping to the ground. My memory is still vivid: skeletal arms flailing, eyes moving in their sockets in what seemed like a silent plea to us, the still living, to help them. But we were powerless. And as they were dying, they defecated. These were dreadful, distressing scenes I didn't fully understand at the time. We were incredulous when we heard that the near-dead would bypass the gas chambers and be placed straight into the crematoria, into the ovens, to burn. Sometimes the dead were left unburied for a time, and eventually inmates who were assigned to this work would come around to collect the cadavers.

These images gave me nightmares for a long time after the Holocaust, and again as I started to speak publicly about what I had witnessed. These are weighty, gruesome memories — difficult to shed, if I ever could.

There was the "shit wagon," as we called it, which came by every day as we stood for roll call. It was used to collect and carry the excrement from the pails that served as toilets around the barracks. Male prisoners pulled these wagons like horses. A reliable rumour had it that the Nazi officers would ask doctors and other professionals and intellectuals to step forward, giving them the impression that they had office jobs for them. In SS fashion, twinning humiliation with deception, these men were assigned to handle the excrement and pull the shit wagon.

At first, we were continually appalled by the new information we learned. However, the shock didn't last, and after a little while we became used to the fact that we were in this dreadful environment.

Those of us in "Mexico" did not work; we were like pigs in a holding pen. On some days, the heat was unbearable. There were no trees under which we could find some shade, some relief. We had to stay outside the barracks during the day, and we were idle and bored, and of course thirsty; there was not enough water to drink, and sunstroke was a serious problem. It is difficult to find the appropriate words to describe our pitiful existence. And yet, as long as we were together, four sisters, we felt fortunate.

Our time was spent talking and sitting around in the dusty outdoors. Occasionally we sang sad melodies. Luckily there were some women with beautiful singing voices. From time to time a few of the women who had managed extensive households in the past spoke, and even boasted, about their cooking and baking skills, even trying to exchange recipes! Hungarian women had a reputation for baking excellent pastries.

After the Holocaust, there was a theory about women in Birkenau and other camps cooking and baking "with their mouths." The theory was that thinking and talking about cooking was a survival tool. I was asked if we young girls enjoyed listening to these conversations about food. My honest answer was no. Some may have felt that these conversations were helpful, but I saw that they were upsetting for the younger women, who felt even hungrier and yearned even more for the unreachable as we listened to them.

Some talented prisoners drew and wrote poetry. But to do so, you needed to somehow get a scrap of paper and a stub of pencil, items that were very difficult to obtain. It was also risky to draw or write, and you could be killed for it. It had to be done quietly, in strict secret — unless you were talented enough to do portraits for the vain SS staff. If the Nazis discovered that you had a special talent they could use, there was a chance it would save your life. I heard that if someone played a musical instrument and was good enough to be accepted in the Auschwitz orchestra, it could mean survival. The musicians mainly played for the entertainment of the SS camp officers but also for the labourers as they marched in and out of the camp to their work sites. Some claim, but I am not sure if it is true, that music was sometimes played at the gruesome time when people were marched into the gas chambers.

One day at the beginning of August, we became aware of something very frightening happening in a camp next to us, in BIIe, known as the "Gypsy family camp," where the Roma were held. There was intense yelling and the barking of SS guards and their dogs, and the screaming and crying of men, women and children as they resisted being evacuated and eventually murdered. I am an earwitness to that event. I heard it all, and I was terribly frightened along with the others in our camp, thinking that we might be gassed next.

We had no calendar, but I think it was a bit later, around the middle of August 1944, that there was another huge selection. Évi and Klári were selected and sent somewhere — we didn't know where. They were in poor condition, especially Klári, but to the camp doctors, they looked healthy enough to work. We cried bitter tears. Thankfully Böske and I were still together, but we were no longer a family. I now slept with Böske in a row with three strangers. Böske was my sole family now, and my guardian angel.

Some of the prisoners in the camp spoke Russian, and they helped my Böske learn the language. We already knew that the Soviet army was coming closer and closer. Böske wanted to be able to tell her liberators in Russian: "Give me work and bread." She taught me that too, and I still remember those Russian words.

Shortly after Évi and Klári were gone, I got sick. I developed arthritis in my hips, which I still suffer from today. I was in terrible, constant pain, and it was difficult for me to stand during roll call. It was also difficult to stand up and sit down. After a while, I just couldn't function. But leaving me in the barracks would mean that I was sick and at risk of being selected to be gassed. And I feared selections more than I feared pain.

Finally, I had no choice. Böske brought me to the *Revier*, the infirmary, and they admitted me. Here, one barely had one's own space. There was one long bunk, and each sick person lay close to the next, almost touching. Sometimes I woke up in the morning to find that the person beside me was dead. Every morning, a nurse and a doctor, both dressed in white, came to examine us. The nurse would take my temperature, and the doctor would look at me and then write something on the card at the foot of the bunk. It was always the same, whether you had a fever or not — you were given two aspirins a day, one in the morning and one at night. As it happens, aspirin is good for curing arthritic pain. But you didn't know at what point those in charge might decide to clear out the *Revier* and send you to the gas chambers. The "death truck," as we called it, with its huge headlights, would come around every single night, throwing frightening shadows on the wall through the windows. The orderlies would come in and pull patients off the bunk, mostly the dead and near-dead ones. I never knew when it might be my turn. This was a singularly terrifying experience.

While I was in the *Revier*, Böske would bring me the extra piece of bread she earned for carrying those heavy food cauldrons. I was reluctant to take it, but she insisted. She didn't want me to lose too much weight and become skinnier than I already was, and she would sit there watching me until I ate every last morsel. I'm sure those slices of bread helped. Most likely she saved my life — once again.

When reflecting back on my time in the *Revier*, I wonder why the Nazis maintained it and seemingly kept accurate records of the patients. Perhaps it is because they wanted to have some kind of proof that they took proper care of the prisoners' health, though it was a deceptive sort of healthcare that they practised, to put it mildly.

After two weeks, I was allowed to leave. I wore the same clothes morning and night, so there was no need to get dressed. As I waited for a guard who would take me back to the barracks, I stood at the window, enjoying the sun shining on my face. When the guard appeared, he started yelling at me, "What are you doing there?!"

"I am enjoying the sunshine," I replied.

Suddenly, he slapped me so hard on the face that I fell to the floor. "You have no right to enjoy the sunshine!" he barked.

This was the only time I recall being beaten by anyone while I was incarcerated. The important thing was that I felt much better — no pain whatsoever. Blessed aspirins!

Our languishing continued as we did nothing and hoped to survive, one day at a time. By then we were used to the worst, though it was hard to get used to the hunger and the fear of separation from Böske, the unyielding hot sun without any shade and seeing the dying and dead around me. But so far, at least Böske and I were still alive. We didn't know what had happened to Évi and Klári, and there was no sense in speculating. We only hoped they were alive somewhere.

～

I was born on the Jewish New Year, Rosh Hashanah, and in 1944, my sweet sixteen birthday was spent in the shadows of the gas chambers, a bitter place indeed. Böske gave me a hug and a kiss, and we celebrated the fact that we were still alive and together. Then came Yom Kippur, the holiest day of the year, and a clandestine and haunting Kol Nidre prayer with the women of Birkenau that would stay with me forever.

Sometime after Yom Kippur, I became extremely ill with high fever, diarrhea and dysentery. I was terribly weak and could not think clearly. As fate would have it, while I was sick, there was another big selection. I don't know the exact date. I vaguely recall that I was selected to go with a group of prisoners, and we were told to sit down, naked, and just wait. I have a hazy memory of seeing Böske far away from me with another group of prisoners, looking in my direction and crying. And I wondered why. Eventually her group had to leave, and she was out of my sight, and I was still sitting there with this group, minus my Böske, my guardian angel. Now I was alone. Fortunately, I didn't comprehend my grave situation. I knew that my good leather shoes had been taken away; they were the only thing I was allowed to keep when we came to Auschwitz, the only thing I still had from home. All of us, all those around me, were without shoes. I didn't understand a thing about what all that meant. I wasn't aware that we were waiting there to be taken to the gas chambers.

I don't know how long we sat there. Finally, a kapo came with some "fresh" dirty clothing and told us to put it on along with some clogs, shoes that had a wooden sole and canvas top. They looked like boots and were heavy and difficult to walk in with our bare feet. But we had to get up and march. Along with the others, I dragged myself to another camp in the Auschwitz-Birkenau complex — the women's compound. We stayed there one night only.

To my great amazement and luck there were two sisters there whom I knew from my home city of Debrecen, Edit and Sári Feig. I had attended middle school with Edit, and Sári, as she would later tell me, had been my brother Miklós's secret and frequent date. I was the same age as Edit, and Sári was seven years older. We were lying beside each other that one night on an upper bunk. They saw how very sick I was and asked me, "Are you alone Jutka?" I answered that I was. Then Sári suggested that the three of us stick together. "Just stay with us," she said. I think Sári took pity on me because I was so sick. But I felt so much safer not being alone.

The next morning, we were put in cattle cars again, and the entire group was taken to the Bergen-Belsen concentration camp in western Germany, near Celle. From then on, Sári, Edit and I became insepa- rable "camp sisters." We stuck together until the very end. "Sistering" with them certainly helped me to get better, and in fact, I recovered completely. A sense of belonging and knowing that someone cared whether I woke up in the morning or not was imperative for sustain- ing my hope and, ultimately, saving my life.

Escaping Fate

Bergen-Belsen was a different ball game. When we arrived there, in October 1944, we lived in tents. The weather was still very nice, there were no gas chambers and the food was better than in Auschwitz. That's not saying much — but it was better.

For breakfast we got something that looked like cream of wheat with milk, and it tasted sweet. It was so unexpected, and we thought that we were really in a good camp. For a short while there was a great improvement in our living conditions. Of course, we were comparing everything to the hell of Auschwitz. Then, the rainy season came, and our tents leaked. The most vivid and bad memories I have of Bergen-Belsen are of soaking wet blankets. The three of us would put our blankets together and huddle under them to warm each other up. But the blankets never had a chance to dry out, and we were constantly covered in damp or wet blankets. My hip started acting up again. As the rainy season continued, life in the camp became dismal. Again, we were idle. No work, nothing to do.

Finally, we were transferred to wooden barracks. But food became more and more scarce. I remember one form of punishment — if they found a piece of straw or something like that on the floor, you didn't get your bread ration. The guards always withdrew food from us as a punishment. Hunger and illness set in, and we became aware that this was not as good a place as it had been when we first arrived. But there was no escape.

I remember the big celebration on New Year's Eve, the end of 1944. Good riddance, we thought! To "celebrate" we received a little extra red cabbage. I don't know why silly things like this stand out in my mind. They are not of any consequence. Things were getting worse, and there was no hope for a better new year. Hunger and a full-blown typhus epidemic were all that were on the horizon.

Early in January 1945, there was a big assembly. Prisoners from different sections of the camp were gathered together. I can still picture the man who spoke to us. He was dressed in civilian clothing, in a beige trench coat and a brown fedora, like one of my brothers used to wear, not in an SS uniform, which was a welcome and reassuring change. It was a cloudy day, and it looked like it was going to rain.

The man spoke in German in a nice, calm tone. He explained that he needed five hundred strong young women to work in his factory, an airplane parts factory called Junkers. The three of us, my camp sisters and I, saw that the conditions in the camp were worsening, and we volunteered to go with him. We decided to present ourselves as three sisters, hoping that would allow us to stay together. I took on their surname and registered myself as Judit Feig, along with Sári Feig and Edit Feig, and we were accepted. All those who volunteered were then assembled and transported by cattle cars to a slave labour camp in the industrial district of Germany, near Leipzig, to a town called Aschersleben. Now we were in the heart of the German war industry, in an area full of ammunition factories.

While we had experienced acute hunger and the brutality of some of the female overseers in Bergen-Belsen, we had escaped the worst. After the war ended, we learned that the typhus epidemic that swept the camp after we left killed many, including the well-known Anne Frank and her sister, Margot, and the corpses were piled high, left unburied. The sick were abandoned and untreated, and Bergen-Belsen turned into a camp of death.

We had escaped that fate by taking a chance on volunteering to work in a place we knew nothing about. This was the first time we had the opportunity to take our fate into our own hands, and it worked out well — as well as could be expected while imprisoned under the brutal Nazi regime.

~

It was January 2, 1945, when we entered the Aschersleben slave labour camp, a subcamp of Buchenwald. Unbelievably, we had decent barracks — decent, of course, compared to Auschwitz-Birkenau's inhuman conditions. We had individual bunk beds with straw mattresses that were covered in white sheets, although annoyingly not without some bedbugs here and there. We even had hot shower facilities at our disposal, and we showered every day. Being able to keep clean was of the utmost importance. We had to be clean in order to maintain morale within the factory. After all, we were now introduced to civil society, so to speak. It was beyond our wildest dreams. Imagine, the barracks were even heated with huge hot-water pipes running right through them. It was hard to believe that we were there.

Our barracks were only a short walk from the factory, which was a blessing as it was bitterly cold outside and we had only very thin coats to wear. The roll calls were dealt with quickly. There was never enough food and we were always hungry, but the food we had was of much better quality than what we were used to. There were actual pieces of meat swimming in the soup at lunchtime, and the bread was tastier than it had been in the other camps. Survival was possible here.

We worked in the factory in rotating shifts alongside hundreds of other workers, some of them Polish and Ukrainian forced labourers who were paid and lived in the town of Aschersleben. I think the majority of them were non-German and many of them were POWs, prisoners of war. Some were Flemish volunteers from Belgium, sympathizers with Nazism. My foreman, Argo, a French POW, warned me about them. He was kind.

Occasionally, we mingled with the others, even though we Jewish women were watched all day long from the gallery above by female SS guards. We were prisoners while working in the privately owned factory. There was perfect coordination and cooperation between the SS and the private war industry in Germany. German industrialists, who employed and exploited, and in most cases sadistically mistreated, their labourers were part and parcel of the Holocaust.

There was also a group of Ukrainian women, over a hundred of them. An interesting scenario developed with the arrival of our group of five hundred Jewish women. The Ukrainians had their own washroom because the German women who worked there would not share their washroom with them. And so, there was a special washroom set up for the workers from the East, with a sign on the door that read, *Ostarbeiter*, Eastern workers. The Ukrainians did not like us, the Jews, and yet the five hundred Jewish prisoners were assigned to use the same washroom as them. They didn't like this situation at all, but they had no choice; the SS made the rules. Eventually we became friendly with these women, and in fact began to engage in a sort of business with them.

There were a number of Jewish women from Czechoslovakia who could converse with the Ukrainian women. The Czech women worked with large pieces of aluminum that they soldered together to create airplane parts. Pieces of scrap aluminum often got left on the floor. Some of these women were very smart, and they secretly used the scrap pieces to make pots and pans. Since they had learned how to solder, they could make lids too. They exchanged these items with the Ukrainian women in the shared washroom: pots and pans for potatoes, carrots or whatever food was available. It was quite a business for those who worked in that area of the factory. Not me. I worked on riveting various kinds of large screws onto the ends of pipes. I hoped to heaven that the planes in which these pipes were placed would never be able to fly. The makers of the pots and pans shared their food with those of us who had nothing to sell.

Unbelievably, I, a Hungarian Jewish girl, saw latkes made for the first time in my life in the barracks of a slave labour camp. In addition to pots and pans, the Czech women made graters by punching many holes into pieces of scrap metal. We all helped grate potatoes and form them into patties, minus eggs of course; but they still stuck together because of the starch from the potatoes. We put the patties on those huge round heating pipes — hot water flowing through them constantly — to "cook" them. When they were ready, the other women yelled out, "Who wants a latke?" "What's a latke?" Edit, Sári and I asked. And so I learned what a latke was in Aschersleben — and I liked it, even though I was told that the real one was much better, with onion, salt and egg, and fried in oil.

While at the Junkers factory, I had a touching experience with one of the young Russian children who also worked there as slaves for twelve hours a day. I surmised that these children had been captured along with their parents after the German army attacked the Soviet Union. One day, one of these children came close to me while I was working and quickly put something wrapped in paper in my hand. This was risky, as the Jewish prisoners were always being watched by the female SS guards. I immediately slipped the item into my pocket. Later I unwrapped it to find a big chunk of hard sugar. It was an incredibly surprising act of generosity. Of course, I shared the sugar with Edit and Sári. I never saw that child again. I don't know what happened to him. That young boy had a heart. I still wonder what he thought of me — that I was hungrier than he was?

My foreman, Argo, saw that sometimes I was very disheartened. The POWs in the factory had access to news reports, but we Jews didn't know what was happening in the war. In a whisper, Argo would try to alleviate my dark mood by singing "La Marseillaise," the French national anthem, when the war reports were good. He would smile at me and sing very quietly so that the SS overseers couldn't hear him. He once also shared with me a piece of chocolate from a Red Cross package that he was supposed to get every month; the SS guards would "divert" most of them.

The town of Aschersleben is situated close to Leipzig and not too far from Torgau, which is just west of the Elbe River, the place where the Allied forces eventually met: the Soviet army from the east, the American army from the west. We worked at Junkers until sometime in late March. At this point in the war, the area was subject to frequent air raids, and often in the course of a day we would have to stop work immediately and run into the bunker under the factory — we Jews under the watchful eyes of our SS guards. They would stand at the entrance of the bunker and count us when we entered and again when we left. Most of the time there was the sound of airplanes overhead but no bombardments, and we were rather annoyed at the Allied forces for inconveniencing us but not attacking!

It was difficult for me to run because my so-called boots were falling apart. The canvas tops were separating from the wooden soles. I was very creative though, and with flexible wires I obtained in the factory, I wove a kind of basket — like a muzzle on an aggressive dog — and put it over the front of my shoes. Odd rags covered my bare feet. Somehow, it all held together while I did my work, standing twelve hours a day. But running in them? That was difficult and painful. Eventually that contraption gave me bloody toes and heels. I remember one occasion when we had to run into the bunker, and one of the SS guards counting us noticed my feet and the muzzles I had fashioned. By then they were breaking up a bit. She started to laugh and pointed to my feet, telling the others to look, and they all started to howl with laughter as they beheld my pain and misery.

Finally, one day the much-awaited attack came. Edit, Sári and I were in the barracks when it happened, having worked the night shift. The planes came so fast that we didn't have time to run from the barracks to the bunkers. Our SS guards were frightened, running around like headless chickens. They were American planes, and the bombing was magnificently accurate. We figured that on the previous passes they were only photographing the terrain. We were so happy that none of us were hurt, we were giggling and laughing. The SS guards could not understand our joy. They said that we were *verrückte*, mad. Obviously, we had different perspectives on this war and its outcome.

We later saw that the whole area had been bombarded and learned that the Junkers factory was damaged and many buildings in Aschersleben were destroyed. The post-bombardment mess was tremendous. The air pressure from the exploding bombs had shattered the windows on the barracks, and we had to be careful walking around, with broken pieces of glass everywhere.

After this major attack we had nowhere to work and we wondered and feared what fate awaited us. We sensed the war was not over yet. After some days of waiting anxiously, a high-ranking SS *Oberscharführer*, senior squad leader, came from Buchenwald with a few other officers to tell us that all of us Jewish women had to leave the camp as there was no longer any work for us. Actually, Aschersleben was one of the places where we could have survived to the very end if they had let us stay. But the officer said that he had orders to take us all to the Buchenwald concentration camp to be executed. "They won't let you survive just like that," he said. This was terrifying news.

Then the officer added, "But I won't do it."

A sigh of relief!

We were assigned two Wehrmacht guards with guns and told to gather our belongings and start marching out of the camp. "Go, just march and go. Just leave," the officer said.

"Where to…?" No answer.

We figured — this was speculation of course — that he saw that the end of the war was near and didn't want to bother with a big job like getting almost five hundred of us to Buchenwald. We suspected that he would report to headquarters that by the time he arrived in Aschersleben, we had all escaped after the bombardment. In any case, he chose to let us go. So we left the camp with a very meagre food supply and started marching on the road to no definite destination other than death by starvation under the watchful eyes of our guards.

The Never-Ending Road

It was a never-ending road, paved with utter, unadulterated misery. My recollections of that time are many but jumbled. Yes, we were, if one can call our dragging ourselves, marching. We went along highways and byways. We went through little towns. We went through small forests — wherever the two guards led us. Food, whatever we took with us from the camp, maybe a bit of bread, was quickly gone. On this unending march we received absolutely nothing, no food or water. We didn't even have the opportunity to relieve ourselves properly. The hunger was unbearable, relentless.

From what I recall nobody called the forced marches that happened toward the end of the war "death marches" at the time they were happening. This was an expression that emerged post-Holocaust because of what took place during those marches; they were extremely cruel.

This was already mid-April 1945, and the war was coming rapidly to an end, the American and Soviet armies approaching from both sides. The area we were in would turn out to be a historic site: the meeting point of the armies. But, of course, at that point, we didn't know or care. I don't know how long we wandered on those roads. Decades later, a German acquaintance who lived in that area of Germany as a young child estimated from some old maps that we had walked about a hundred kilometres — not in a straight line of course — from Aschersleben to Düben.

As we walked through the forests, we saw corpses that looked like us — wearing ragged clothing — but filled with bullet holes. A rumour was going around that death squads, *Totenkopfverbäende*, in their black uniforms were free to roam around and do whatever they liked. Sometimes they met people like us and just shot them.

Words fail me in describing our absolute desperation. Some prisoners suffered exhaustion, and those of us who grew too weak to carry on were left behind. I didn't see our two guards shoot anybody. Still, we were fewer and fewer as we marched on. Some may have left our group to hide.

When we went through little towns, we would forage in large garbage cans like starving animals, and when we went through open fields or along the highway, we would sometimes run into the fields, hoping something was growing there. I remember some of us digging with our fingers and finding tiny carrots or potatoes. We ate them as they were, muddy.

The most bizarre memories of this march are from when we went through these towns. It was absolutely surreal. Just a few metres from us, we saw normal life, the kind we still remembered, where children went to school, adults went to work, and there were nicely trimmed gardens and cute curtains on the windows of the homes — while we were marching, wrapped in rags, filthy, dirty and starving. We saw them; they looked, but they didn't really see us. They did their best to ignore our pitiful, bedraggled group. Decades later, I saw videos in the new Bergen-Belsen Memorial Museum in Germany in which ordinary Germans were interviewed and said that the authorities told them not to open their doors to people marching through because they were all criminals. "So we were afraid of them," they said.

One day, something quite unforgettable happened. As we were dragging ourselves along the shoulder of the highway in one direction, we saw, on the other side of the highway, a group of soldiers marching in the opposite direction. I had never seen dark-skinned people before. Their uniforms were in various stages of tatters, and some of them wore white turbans. This was such an unusual sight to us, we could not easily forget it. We stopped in our tracks to watch and were mortified by what we witnessed. These P O W s were guarded by vicious soldiers who held huge horsewhips and whipped the men mercilessly to hurry them along. By then, we Jewish prisoners had seen and experienced a lot of brutality. And yet, I am glad to recall that we remained humane enough to still be horrified at this display of senseless sadism. We were aware that something was wrong with this situation, that the P O W s should have been protected by an international agreement. My memory of this day and of humans being beaten by horsewhips will never fade. Decades later, I discovered that these were most likely Sikh soldiers from India who were in the British army, and some of them may have been from Tunisia.

As we continued marching, my feet became a bloody mess in the contraptions I wore, which were now unrecognizable as boots. Walking was extremely painful. The three of us began propping each other up, alternately holding up the one of us who was giving up hope.

One day, sheer desperation took hold of us, and Sári and Edit said to me, "Let's start begging. You look the most pitiful of the three of us, so you beg." I had no mirror to confirm this, and in any case, hunger trumped vanity and I agreed.

As we went through one of these neat little towns, I stepped out of the line and knocked on the door of a home. I clearly recall its green door. The woman of the house opened it and looked at me with shock. Trembling, I quickly told her in German that I had been walking from Aschersleben and that I was very hungry; could she please give me something to eat. She just kept looking at me, then said in German, "Warten Sie" (Wait). She turned around, and when she came back, she was holding what looked to my hungry eyes like a very large slice of bread. It was loaded with marmalade. She quickly closed the door before I had time to say "Danke" (Thank you), perhaps because I smelled bad. Fast as I could, I caught up with the moving line and shared every morsel of that treasure with Sári and Edit.

Every night when we happened to be in a small town, our guards would ask the mayor to let us sleep in an empty barn. There were many empty barns because the German farmers in this area didn't know which army would reach their town first — the Americans or the Soviets. They feared the Russian soldiers terribly, and many families just up and left. Most of the time, the mayors refused, and we had to lie down under the sky and stars on the outskirts of town.

The day after the feast of bread and marmalade, evening came, and the mayor of the town we had come to permitted us to use a large abandoned barn to sleep in. There was a thin layer of straw on the earthen floor. By now our numbers had dwindled considerably. We were hungry and exhausted and without eating or drinking, we lay down on the ground and fell asleep.

The next morning, we were awakened from our shallow sleep by a loud knock on the barn door. Disoriented and startled, we quickly sat up. Someone opened the door, and there stood a tall man in the doorway, the sunshine behind him. All we could see was his dark silhouette. In a pleasant, strong voice he addressed us in German: "Fräulein!" We were astonished. It was absolutely unheard of that a German would address us in a civil manner. We were used to being called everything: *verfluchte Juden*, accursed Jews, or *dreckige Juden*, dirty Jews — all sorts of degrading names. My two camp sisters and I looked at each other: *Did he really say "Fräulein"?* We concluded that the war must be over and started to cry. Then the man continued, "Fräulein, Sie sind frei" (Young ladies, you are free). That was our first liberation. The man, who was the mayor of the town, asked us all to come outside. We looked around and saw white flags on all the homes, no swastikas anywhere. No trumpets or confetti either — just three quiet, magnificent words: You are free. It was a beautiful sunny day.

Chaotic Freedom

The mayor, true to Nazi form, was without compassion though. He didn't offer us any food — not even a drink of water. I think he wanted to get rid of us as quickly as he could. He told us that we were free to leave (of course, our guards had disappeared) and that we should continue on our way, offering us this explanation: "There are two roads you can follow from here." As he pointed, he said, "If you take this road, ten kilometres from here are the Russians. If you take that road, six kilometres from here are the Americans."

Within seconds we all decided — six is less than ten, so we would go to the Americans. Those four extra kilometres determined where we would end up. The word liberation meant Life-With-Hope to us. We were so relieved, like a heavy burden had been lifted — the burden of constant fear — and that energized us to drag ourselves six kilometres to the next town, Düben. We had a goal, a destination!

At one point on the way, we spotted a khaki-coloured truck coming toward us. We worried that it was another kind of SS division that we didn't recognize. But as it came closer, we saw the Red Cross symbol. Some soldiers got off the truck as soon as they saw us, and they were flabbergasted at the sight of our group. We must have been some sight. In halting German, we let them know who we were: liberated Jewish prisoners of the Nazis, and very hungry. Right away, each of them dug into their pockets and gave us something wrapped in paper

— chewing gum. We were unfamiliar with gum, and we didn't know if we should swallow it or spit it out. It was quite hilarious.

They told us to continue walking, that it wasn't far to Düben. We marched on with renewed energy. Once we were with the American military we felt secure, truly liberated. A Jewish military chaplain was waiting for us in Düben. One of the Red Cross members had obviously radioed that a group of Jews was arriving. The chaplain had little mezuzahs for us to hang around our necks as a welcome gift. It was a nice gesture, but at that point a big slice of bread would have been more beneficial. We were disappointed. Mezuzahs hanging from our necks did not subdue our hunger.

The chaplain told us that it was Saturday, May 5, and the war was still going on. In another three days, Germany would capitulate, and the war would officially be over.

The American military officials were stunned and perplexed by our arrival and by the condition we were in. They were not ready for a group like us. How could they be equipped to deal with two hundred starving Jewish women? They kindly explained that they could give us accommodation right away because the SS officers' barracks were available. So we had the military barracks, which were rather nice and comfortable, our home for the time being. There were clean white sheets on every mattress and hot water facilities in which we could shower away the filth that covered our bodies. In a way we wanted to get cleaned up even more than we wanted to eat.

The military leaders admitted that they had no idea how to provide meals for hundreds of women. Besides, the war was still going on. The commandant said that all they could do was allow us to fend for ourselves. We were permitted to walk into any store in the town and take food, clothing or other items we needed and wanted, without paying for them. There were American soldiers and military police with large identifying armbands constantly patrolling the streets. We were told that if we had problems with the staff or owners of the stores to just call upon any police officer on the street to help. Well, this was a very bad plan. What we really needed was hospitalization, to be checked out, and to eat very light food to start with. But at that point the Americans couldn't provide us with that.

Our presence became known very quickly, and the inhabitants of Düben didn't resist our approaches. Well, at least we were relatively clean and smelled good from the soap we were given in the barracks.

The free-for-all worked up to a point, then it became chaotic. I clearly remember Sári, Edit and I walking into a grocery store that had been abandoned, looking for sugar. We yearned for sugar. We went into the back room where most of the items were stored. Here the Germans had food — lots of it. They could have supplied the Americans. There were large bags of sugar, but they were too heavy for our weak arms to lift. So, we just tore them apart, and right there and then we gobbled the granulated sugar, scooping it with our hands. We ate and ate, a lot of it pouring onto the floor, but we didn't care; we walked on sugar. Some of the others went into butcher stores and lifted huge salamis and other deli meats off the meat hooks, and some of the women walked into bakeries and took bread and buns, way beyond what was enough. We just wanted to get whatever we could put our hands on and gorge ourselves. We were like hungry animals.

The food that people collected was brought into the barracks, where we shared it. Unfortunately, the end result was that most of us got very sick eating the wrong food like salami and fresh bread, and lots of it. We had diarrhea from all that food that we should not have eaten. Now there was a new problem! Where were we going to get toilet paper? Someone had a bright idea: *Let's rob a bank and use bank notes.* That was said and done. Another unexpected disappointment! The Reichsmark banknotes were printed on large sheets of stiff paper — not usable for our purpose. We were in a quandary. I think we probably found old newspapers and used that.

On May 8 came the armistice. Germany had capitulated. The war was over. We were told that the free-for-all, which had lasted three days by now, had to stop. Happily, by that time the military had started to get organized and was paying attention to us and our needs. Those who needed medical treatment were taken care of. I needed treatment for my feet. Somehow clean clothing was obtained and we received proper shoes. I remember one of the new garments I received was a pair of trousers that you could bind under the knees. Young men wore pants like that in those days. They were called breeches, and they were stylish. I also was given a blouse, nothing fancy, and clean underwear. That was very important.

Now we truly felt liberated. There was nothing ecstatic or Rah! Rah! Rah! about it. But the heaviest weight was lifted from our shoulders and minds: fear for our lives. We weren't hungry anymore, and we knew that every day we'd have three meals. At that point, we mainly saw liberation as it pertained to our physical needs. Other problems and issues came later. For now, we were starting to recover and slowly become what I called born-again human beings.

One morning about a month later, as we got up and looked out the window of our barracks, we noticed soldiers in unfamiliar uniforms walking around. We were fearful of changes and wondered anxiously who they were. One of the girls from Czechoslovakia said, "Oh, these are the Russians."

An agreement had been made between the Allies to divide Germany up into zones, and the area we were in was now part of the Soviet Zone, which eventually became Communist East Germany. On this morning, the Americans, our liberators, were gone, and suddenly Düben belonged to the Soviets. For us, it meant new people and a new authority to get used to. Some of the Czech women who were with us spoke Russian and could communicate with the soldiers.

A few of them came over to get acquainted with us and brought their small round accordions, *harmoshkas* as they called them, and sang beautiful songs. They had wonderful voices and some of them were really very handsome. But a serious problem also developed.

We learned that the Soviet soldiers were coming straight from the front, most likely very angry, and that they were taking the liberty of raping women, mainly German women, but any woman would do. I think it was on the second night that some of the soldiers came to our barracks, very drunk, and wanted to have sex with us, even forcefully. We were jumping out through the windows to escape from them. Luckily, we had a short way to jump from the ground floor. At first we were scared, then outraged. We definitely did not want to be raped.

The morning after this incident, a few girls went to the Soviet military command to complain. The Czech girls explained in Russian what had happened. The soldiers received very strict instructions not to touch us, and it never happened again. They did come visit again, but it was during the day and with their *harmoshka*s. They sang and we hummed along to the melodies. It was very pleasant, and we became friendly with those few who just wanted to socialize with us.

One day, one of the soldiers asked the Czech girls to come along with him to get wine from some of the German inhabitants. He was sure they all had wine in their homes. I went along because I wanted to see what would happen. We went from house to house, five or six of us. One house in particular stands out in my mind. A very old German man came to the door. When he saw the Soviet soldier, he was scared. The Czech girls translated from Russian and told the man that the soldier wanted wine. The old man kept saying, "Ich hab keine, keine" (I have none, none). When the girls translated the German to the soldier, he got angry, took out his pistol, pointed it at the old man and yelled, "Vino! Vino!" Finally, the man went downstairs to his cellar and came up with four bottles of wine, which he handed to us. The soldier turned to us and asked, "Should I shoot him anyway?" "No, no," we replied, and we all left. We saved that old man.

One really has to understand the context for the anger that was in the hearts of the Soviet soldiers. It was a response to what the Germans had done in their country — the devastation of so much land. As the Germans retreated, they burned everything in a strategy called scorched-earth policy. The Soviet soldiers had a hatred for the Germans that was probably equal to the Nazis' hatred of them. Even similar to ours. The Americans didn't have the same hatred toward the Germans because America itself was not invaded, harmed or destroyed. Those who were killed were the heroic US soldiers fighting abroad in the fields, in the sky or on ships, on the battlefronts.

We spent maybe two weeks with the Soviets, but they didn't have displaced persons (DP) camps. Those who they liberated were allowed to return to their home countries right away if they were healthy enough to make that rough journey, often on foot. A good number of displaced persons returned to Hungary or Czechoslovakia or wherever they came from on their own. There must have been some agreement between the Soviet and American military administrations because one day a few American military trucks arrived and moved us all to Leipzig, the nearest big city, where there was a large DP camp for numerous refugees from different countries, Jews and non-Jews. Here, we were told, we could figure out where to go next.

And that's what happened. We remained in Leipzig for a number of weeks. We were encouraged to explore the city by the tramway, which was free; we didn't have money anyway. We were told we didn't have to pay for any service. The local Germans in Leipzig learned very quickly who we were. Our presence made them uncomfortable. When we travelled among them on the tramway, they would try to defend themselves, claiming that they didn't know anything about what had happened. One person said to me, "Aber Hitler war ein lumpen!" (But Hitler was a rag!), meaning, a nobody. We didn't say anything to them. We didn't accuse them of anything, yet, sitting beside us, they felt compelled to defend themselves just the same. Who could believe them? The slave labour camps and factories were in the area, not that far from Leipzig, which was the heart of industrial Germany. There had been ammunitions factories and airplane-parts factories. They knew of the slaves who were working in them. There was no way they didn't know. Many of them had worked alongside

Jews and other slaves in those factories. We knew they were lying. None of us knew German well enough to get into a meaningful discussion. We just laughed because we didn't believe them and they felt they had to defend themselves. Deep down, I am sure they knew they were, one way or another, complicit with the Nazi authorities.

In time, we were registered as refugees, and each of us had to decide where we would like to go, where to get on with our shattered lives. These were the days when we had to face the stark reality head on. We had to look into our future and ask: *Where to? How to? Why go on living at all?*

We were no longer hungry. We weren't thirsty. We had clothing. We weren't sick. There was no danger. We no longer needed to be preoccupied with our physical and material needs. This is when our psychological anguish set in.

I was sixteen and a half years old — and possibly all alone in the world. I didn't know if I was the only survivor from my family. Did I still belong to anyone?

Fearful, heart-wrenching questions and doubts.

At this point we heard that Sweden was accepting some survivors and that France had opened up refugee camps for young people. Sári, Edit and I were discussing where to go, vacillating. In the end, we thought our best bet was to go back to Hungary to find out who else was alive.

I knew who was *not* coming back: my parents; my sister-in-law, Magda, and my nephew, Péter; Aunt Sarolta. Uncle Vilmos had died of cancer before the deportation. But I reasoned and felt deep down that if I, the youngest of seven siblings, had survived, then surely all my older siblings had too, and most likely they would be heading home as well. The most reasonable place to meet would be in Debrecen.

So, that was what we decided. The Americans were surprised by our decision. "You want to go back to the same country that kicked you out?" they asked. Some people thought that we were absolutely insane to go back there. But it seemed like the most logical thing for us to do at that point.

As it turned out, logic didn't play a big role in who got murdered and who, by sheer luck, survived.

An Exchange of Tragedies

Travelling home in the summer of 1945 was a rather arduous, unpleasant journey in war-torn, bombed-out, chaotic Central Europe. I was very anxious about what I might find when I got home, but I hoped. I kept telling myself over and over that if I had survived, then surely all my older and smarter siblings would have too.

We were driven to the border of Czechoslovakia in military trucks along with quite a few others who were going back to their homes. I have scant memory of the entire trip, probably because I was traumatized, and I later relied on Sári and Edit to recall this period. I know we travelled through Czechoslovakia on a train for a while. Then we were sidetracked while more important trains went through, some with American or Soviet soldiers — victorious liberators or occupiers, depending on one's outlook. We saw, as the train finally moved again, lots of buildings in ruins. I can't recall how we obtained food. The Americans must have supplied us with some Czech money. Sadly, Sári and Edit are no longer among the living to further jog my memory about this journey.

Finally, we arrived in Budapest. By this time, the Jewish community there was well organized; they had been liberated by the Soviet army a number of months earlier, in January and February 1945. A Jewish committee registered us, and they wanted to know who I was, where I came from, and then, where did I want to go? They asked

Edit and Sári the same questions. I told them that I wanted to go back to Debrecen, so they telephoned an office there and gave them our names. Debrecen's Jewish community was also organized by then.

We stayed in Budapest for two or three days and met up with my cousins Olga and Jenö Mandel, who were very nice to us. We slept in group homes for those few days, and then we were put on a train to Debrecen. Needless to say, it was a very anxious trip from Budapest to Debrecen. We arrived at the station and, of course, nobody was waiting for me or for the Feig sisters. Since we lived in different parts of the city, my camp sisters and I had to part ways. We cried and hugged; it was difficult to say goodbye.

As I walked to my old house from the station alone, my heart was heavy, loaded with terrible memories and dreadful knowledge, and yet it was also hopeful. Walking on the well-known Széchenyi utca, on which I had walked with friends almost daily, I recalled how much I used to enjoy the abundance of acacia trees that exuded a delicate perfume. Now it seemed desolate and surreal, like it had been eons since I was here the last time. I had experienced many lifetimes between then and now. And here I was, walking home from hell on earth. I had wished for and dreamed of this moment so many times while languishing in the dust of Birkenau.

Finally, I turned the corner onto my street, Nyugati utca. It also seemed old, rundown and ugly, uninviting. Suddenly, as I looked up, I saw two men walking toward me. As we got closer, I recognized Laci, the youngest of my three brothers, and our cousin Ernö Klein! It was a joy and relief to see them. I was no longer alone. Laci looked gaunt and pale; he had just recovered from typhus, he told me. Ernö was in good condition. They had both returned to Debrecen from forced labour battalions a while before I returned to Hungary, and they were living in our old house. We hugged and cried right there on the street. Then we walked back to the place that had been our home.

We reached Nyugati utca 34 and that large, heavy iron door I remembered so well, then into the courtyard that looked terribly neglected and, finally, our dwelling. Everything seemed so very strange. Our furniture was all gone, and nothing was cozy or familiar. Yet, here is where I broke down and cried uncontrollably. It was here where the enormity of the Holocaust dawned on me. Not in the camps, where the priority was just survival. Not in the refugee camp, where getting back to normalcy, feeling like a human being again, occupied my life. It was here where my colossal losses stared me in the face, where my future looked utterly sad and bleak. In fact, I saw no future. At this moment, I faced the inevitable and difficult questions and struggled to answer them.

Our understanding of the historical facts slowly unfolded. As fate had it, Debrecen, from where we had been deported on June 29, 1944, was liberated by the Soviet army on October 19, 1944 — a mere three and a half months between survival and mass murder. About half of the 13,000 Jews in the Debrecen ghettos had been deported to Auschwitz-Birkenau, and the other half to Strasshof, Austria. They turned out to be the lucky ones. While they too endured hardships, hunger and plenty of brutality, they never faced the lethal gas chambers and the other deadly processes of the death camps, which were specially built for the mass annihilation of Jews and others.

Thankfully, most of those deported to Austria remained alive. In some cases, entire families were intact and had been able to get back to Hungary almost immediately at the war's end. We learned that this group from Debrecen was part of the "blood for trucks" negotiations between the Jewish leadership of Hungary, the mayor of Vienna and Eichmann, who agreed to allow approximately twenty thousand Hungarian Jews to be sent to Austria to fill labour needs there in exchange for money and valuables. Once back, these survivors were able to establish a well-functioning Jewish community and started helping others who were returning.

When I returned home, it seemed to me that many in Debrecen still did not know about Auschwitz-Birkenau and the other death camps. All they knew was what the Jews who had survived in Austrian captivity had told them. When the Auschwitz-Birkenau survivors started trickling back to Debrecen, even my relatives who had been in forced labour battalions were totally ignorant of the fact that there had been two very different deportation destinations; they thought all Jews from Debrecen had been deported to Austria. Then I came along, one of the first to return from the death camps and one of the few survivors. I told Laci about how our mother and father, our sister-in-law, Magda, and our infant nephew, Péter, were all murdered in the gas chambers of Birkenau, most likely shortly after our arrival and the first selections.

"Don't wait for them, Laci, they will never come back," I said.

Three male cousins, Miklós Ehrenfeld, and Simi and Jenö Kohn, wanted to know about their wives and young daughters. I was the bearer of devastating news, that their beloved wives and young daughters had all been murdered in the gas chambers of Birkenau.

They were shocked. Gas chambers? They didn't believe me. They thought I was raving mad. I also explained what "selections" meant in a death camp and how eventually we four sisters — Évi, Klári, Böske and I — were separated in two stages, and that I had no idea where they might be or even if they were alive. Laci didn't believe me. Still, he felt devastated.

I frequently broke into uncontrollable crying, weighed down by all the agonizing memories and the irreversible reality of my great losses. I had to bottle up all my nightmarish memories. Nobody wanted to hear such incredibly horrible, unbelievable stories. Those were emotionally heavy and difficult days and weeks for me, and it was hard for others to fathom what I was going through or what had happened. There was nowhere to turn for solace.

The unprecedented, brutal facts about what had happened surfaced slowly and were released by the media over the next decade. In Communist countries like Hungary, the process was even slower. The prominence of Jewish victims was underplayed, and the stories about the victims of fascists in Budapest and its vicinity were emphasized.

The scope and enormity of the industrial-style mass murder didn't become well known worldwide until the Eichmann trial in Jerusalem, which began on April 11, 1961. That late! Until then, few knew the extent of this genocide, or the *Churban*, Destruction, as the Jews referred to it until the word "Holocaust" was popularized in the 1950s and '60s. It took fifty years for the Hungarian government to create a Holocaust memorial and museum in Budapest in 2004.

Laci's story of survival surfaced slowly as we spent more time together. He and some of my cousins had been in different forced labour battalions with the Hungarian army and had somehow survived. Laci's liberation, by the Soviet Red Army in Austria, was nothing short of a miracle.

In Laci's words, a mere three minutes had made the difference between life and death. Sick with typhus, he and the others in the unit had been abandoned by their Hungarian fascist guards somewhere in Austria. They found an empty schoolroom and lay down on the floor to rest. Suddenly, a Waffen SS soldier arrived on a motorcycle, and surmising from the condition they were in that they were Jews, he took out his gun to shoot them. At that moment, his comrade roared in on a motorcycle, breathless and yelling in German, "Fritz komm doch, schnell, die Russen sind da!" (Fritz, come fast, the Russians are here!), and they both fled, not having time to kill anyone.

The Soviet military helped Laci and his group get healthy and sent them home once they were strong enough to walk. However, when they finally crossed into Hungary, they were stopped by Soviet or Ukrainian military police and told to identify themselves. The police were looking for Arrow Cross fascists who were trying to escape justice. Nobody in the group had ID cards, so they were arrested as members of the Arrow Cross and put in an internment camp together with fascists, whom the Soviet military planned to send to Siberia. Needless to say, the Jewish men did not want to end up in Siberia. They were not guilty of anything; they were the victims. Every day, a few of them pleaded with the military officials to let them go free.

Luckily, one day the chief military official was replaced, and the new one was a Russian Jew who listened to their plea, made sure they were really Jewish and let them go free. It would have been a terrible fiasco if Laci and the others had ended up in Siberia.

Laci had terribly sad news for me regarding my two oldest brothers, Jenö and Miklós. He heard that Miklós had been killed at Voronezh, where there was a major military battle and thousands of Hungarian and Soviet troops were slaughtered, though Miklós was there as a slave labourer, not as a combatant. And Jenö was murdered by Hungarian officers in Doroshich. The Hungarians had marched into Ukraine as allies of Nazi Germany, and the Jewish slaves had to go along with the army. Jews were sent to the front lines in case there were minefields; they were the canaries in the coal mine, the cannon fodder. In addition, they were brutally treated by this particular division, the Hungarian Second Army.

This is what we learned, and it was later validated by the Hungarian government: As the Hungarian Second Army was retreating from the Soviets, about four hundred Jewish slaves got sick with typhoid fever. They were quarantined in a makeshift hospital in the town of Doroshich. Instead of taking these sick men with them, the officers burned down the hospital with the Jewish men in it. It was a massacre. A few men managed to crawl out unnoticed and were witnesses to what happened. My oldest brother was among those murdered. There were several Weissenberg cousins and numerous other Jews from Debrecen who were in that division and perished. Only a few of my cousins returned from the Hungarian slave labour battalions.

My welcome home, it seems, was the exchange of utterly tragic stories. The bleak picture unfolded: Our parents; at least some of our siblings; our little nephew, Péter; Magda; and numerous aunts, uncles and cousins had all been murdered one way or another. We were told that Jenö had known that he had a son but never had the chance to hold him.

Each of these relatives was murdered in a particular hell of the Holocaust. But there was still hope for our three sisters, that they were alive somewhere in Europe, since there was no definitive news about them. I told Laci what I knew about what had happened to them while we were still in Auschwitz. I guessed that Évi and Klári had been taken somewhere else, but I didn't know where Böske ended up because she was still in Birkenau when I was taken away. At home we just waited and constantly checked the lists of survivors.

Laci and two of my cousins had been living in our home for a while by now, and had created a new family unit. We had the basic necessities from the Jewish community's furniture bank, an abandoned furniture store. So there were beds, tables and chairs, though none of the furniture matched, and it didn't feel like ours. But we were all happy to be alive and have some kind of a home.

～

By the time I returned to Debrecen in early August 1945, the Jewish high school I had once attended no longer existed. It had been combined with a non-denominational state high school. The school board allowed the few of us who returned to complete the grade we missed if we could finish by the end of September. Continuing our education was important, and so I went back to school. I was going on seventeen, and it was a good distraction from wrestling with my agonizing memories and traumatic experiences. There I rejoined a couple of my former classmates, Anci and Agi, and a few others who had survived in Austria with their entire families intact, ignorant of all my terrible experiences. We were all trying to make up for the missing year. I still have documentation that shows that I finished one grade in six weeks. Admittedly, the teachers were very lenient in their expectations.

Going back to school, I had some kind of a life, though not much of one. I didn't have many friends from the old days because most of them had died in Auschwitz. Anci and Agi moved to Budapest, and so did Edit and Sári, to join their brother there. As the new school year started, I enrolled in my last year of high school.

⁓

I think it was November or December of 1945 when a young lady knocked on our door and asked, "Is there anybody from the Weissenberg family alive here?" "Yes, we are," Laci answered. Then she said, "Here," and handed us a small piece of paper. On it was just a name, "Weissenberg, Évi," and our address, in my sister's handwriting. This most welcome stranger then told us that Évi was alive; they had been liberated together! Évi was still recovering, and after being in the hospital for a long time, she was now convalescing in the Bergen-Belsen DP camp in Germany. The young lady explained that when she had decided to head back to Transylvania via Debrecen, Évi begged her to look up this address and tell whoever she found that she was alive and where she was. It was very kind of her to stop and look us up. She gave us the most welcome, happy news. Now we were three.

But we had not yet heard any news of Böske and Klári.

At that time my brother had connections with the Zionist underground, the Bricha, which had a mission to help survivors get to British Mandate Palestine. Travel in Europe was still very chaotic, and illegal unless you had official papers. So my brother signed up with the Bricha, but he didn't tell them that he was not going to Palestine. He told them that he first wanted to get to his sister and only after that go to Palestine.

When Laci finally got to Bergen-Belsen and joined Évi, he told her that he had come to take her back to Debrecen, but she did not want to leave. She was too weak to travel, and she had a boyfriend. She was a beautiful girl, twenty years old by then. As far as she had known, she was alone, and she had not searched for family except for that note she sent to Debrecen with her friend. When my brother told her that I was alive and at home, she thought that he was lying.

"What are you talking about? Jutka was gassed in Birkenau. She's not alive."

"You are wrong. She's at home," Laci assured her.

Still, Évi didn't want to come home. She said that she didn't want to see Hungary ever again. I think it was also because she had a boyfriend who looked after her very nicely. He was a very good-looking man from Riga, Latvia, who had lost his wife and two children in the Holocaust. He was at least ten years older than Évi, around thirty years old. In the DP camps there were many single people who had lost all their family; they were lonely and yearning for companionship, to belong to someone, to anyone. Many marriages took place between lonely people who would not have been a match under normal circumstances. Weddings, marriages and then of course came the children in a remarkable renewal of family life, renewal of life itself.

Laci returned from Germany without Évi. He told me all sorts of fairy tales about what would happen if we went back to Germany. I told him that I wanted to matriculate first. "No," he said, "we are not waiting. We will go back to Germany, and in six months' time we will have a chance to leave Europe. We'll settle down somewhere else." I told him that I wasn't going. But he was bugging me, bugging me, bugging me. He won.

Slow Recovery

In early 1946, two months after Laci came back from Germany, we left Hungary with the Bricha. We were young, foolish, stubborn and inexperienced, and like many young people at that time, bereft of wise parental advice. You sometimes don't know how foolish your decisions are. Even my cousins urged Laci to let me finish my high school education. The big draw in leaving of course was that we three siblings would be together. And Laci insisted that our goal was to leave Europe, that it was no longer a place for Jews, and he didn't want to go to Palestine at that point.

Finally, he convinced me that we had to move on, and we left Hungary illegally. We packed up, and whatever we could not take along we left behind. We left some precious items with our cousin Böske Klein, Ernö's sister, who eventually ended up in Buenos Aires, Argentina.

Years later, my cousin Böske came to visit us in Toronto and brought us one of the items we had left behind in 1946 — a sterling silver sugar or salt holder, a wedding present to my parents, beautifully engraved with the date June 10, 1910. It is my second most sacred memento of a life we once enjoyed and cherished. My first sacred memento is my mother's personal prayer book, which she received from my father on their wedding day. It contains a beautiful dedication to her in Hungarian, written in excellent calligraphy. It had been buried with some silver items until Laci dug them up after the war, and the pages were yellowed with time and the cover was damaged from moisture. And yet it is still the most precious item I own. I hope it will be buried with me.

We started our journey back to Germany. That was an unusual voyage! As we crossed borders, we and the others we travelled with had to lie on the floor of trucks and be absolutely quiet so that we would not be discovered. The Bricha leaders knew which border guards to bribe, using the money they had collected from us. It was all very clandestine. I couldn't help thinking, as I lay on the floor of the truck: *I survived Auschwitz and other horrors, do I need this, leaving home again in this humiliating manner?* Indeed, I thought it was crazy. During the months I was in Hungary, some of the socialist ideas I was learning about appealed to me, and I had begun to feel comfortable there. To leave behind everything that was slowly becoming familiar again was madness, sheer madness!

I don't remember why, but we got stuck in Vienna, and there we parted ways with the Palestine-bound group. As it turned out, the weeks we were in Vienna left me with new, unexpected and enriching experiences. We stayed in a home for refugees, and we were free to roam and explore the city. For a while, there were no major worries, and I had a temporary rest from thinking about my recent past or contemplating my uncertain future. At seventeen, under the right circumstances, life seemed promising. Vienna was where I saw my first opera, *La bohème*, in the Volksoper theatre because the state opera house, the Staatsoper, had been bombed and was not yet restored.

This was also the first time I went to a nightclub, and it didn't turn out so well. I had a little liquor, I drank a little wine. I had a little of everything. It didn't take much to get me drunk. The other guys urged my brother to take me home. I remember when we stepped outside and the fresh air hit me, I became unsteady, fell onto my knees and tore my only pair of silk stockings. That's all I cared about, that I tore my stockings. In those days, stockings were a treasure! When we returned to our room, Laci just threw me onto the upper bunk bed, fully dressed, shoes and all, and then went back to the nightclub. He never took me to a club again.

After that episode, I explored Vienna and Schönbrunn with some newly made friends from the home for refugees. We walked around a lot, visiting beautiful parts of the city and finding places to drink delicious coffee. My new friends were from Budapest and were making the same journey as us. These friends were modern and with-it. They had brought a record player along with them, and I had the thrill of listening for the first time to the song "Begin the Beguine," by Cole Porter. This song has always reminded me of that time in Vienna.

Eventually we found a connection who could get us to Germany, and we left Vienna and our transient life behind.

~

The reunion with Évi was incredibly emotional, more so than the one with my brother. I think it was the joy of seeing each other again and recalling the traumatic moment of selection in Birkenau that had torn us sisters apart — an instantly familiar shared memory. But Évi kept repeating, "Jutka, you are right here with me, and I still can't believe that you are alive." For two weeks she was pinching me to make sure. She wanted to know what had happened. I told her what I remembered: Sitting naked with all the others selected to be gassed, which I hadn't known then, and Böske looking in my direction, crying; how I was sick and didn't understand why Böske was crying; then, Böske's group marching back to the barracks. And we never saw each other again. Then I and the group I was with were taken to the Bergen-Belsen concentration camp. I don't know why we weren't gassed. After the war, we learned that toward the end of 1944 they sometimes ran out of Zyklon B gas, and this may have been the reason for this modern-day "miracle."

I asked Évi if she knew what had happened to Böske and Klári. Évi took over the story.

In August 1944, when Klári and Évi were selected out of Auschwitz-Birkenau, they were taken to another terrible camp called Stutthof, also in Poland. Évi cried as she began telling me what happened. They had a rough time of it, especially Klári. She developed big sores on her body from malnutrition and was slowly going blind. Évi knew that Klári needed more food to get better, so she volunteered, along with about thirty other women from Stutthof, to work in a factory in town where they mended torn German uniforms. They were escorted there by guards in the morning and back in the evening. There Évi had a chance to interact with Polish workers with whom she began to barter: for her bread ration, she could obtain cigarettes and sewing needles from some of the male POWs, which she then bartered for potatoes, carrots or whatever vegetables the Polish women brought to the factory.

Évi and the other prisoners did this as long as they could. They smuggled these items into the camp by hiding them between the lining and cloth of their coats. Évi would give the vegetables to Klári, even though there was often no way to cook them, so she ate them raw. Then, in the fall of 1944, a new transport came to Stutthof from Auschwitz, and to my sisters' immense surprise and dubious joy, Böske was among them. Böske told them that the last time she saw me, I was among those who were going to be gassed. And so the sisters cried and said Kaddish in their own way and continued the struggle to survive, Böske and Évi focusing on helping Klári.

Évi suddenly stopped at this point in her story. "I will tell you something now, but only once," she said. "Please, don't ask me about it ever again."

One day, when the group of women that Évi was with was coming back from the factory, the guards lined them up against the fence. That had never happened before, and the women sensed that something was amiss. Each of them faced one SS guard with an SS-trained dog. Suddenly, the dogs were let loose to attack the women. These were killer dogs, and the women were terrified. Even as Évi told this story, remembering the scenes, her eyes bulged with fear, as if she were living through it again.

The dogs started tearing at the women's coats and clothing, the hidden vegetables falling out one by one, their clothing in tatters around their legs, their naked bodies bleeding. They expected the dogs to go for their jugulars and kill them right there and then. But by a sudden command, the dogs were called off.

After this incident, Évi didn't have a chance to smuggle any more food to Klári or Böske, who was also getting thin and weak and had contracted pneumonia.

By this point in her story, Évi was crying uncontrollably, pleading, "Jutka, please believe me, I really tried to save them both but could not. They both starved to death, practically in my arms." I kept hugging and kissing her, assuring her through my tears that I believed her implicitly. Her survival story was horrific too.

As the Soviet army approached Stutthof, it was evacuated. The group Évi was with was taken to the Baltic Sea and put on barges that started to float away. There were some male Norwegian prisoners among them who had been incarcerated years before as Communists, and they told the rest of the group to jump into the water because the SS planned to blow up the barges. Évi could not swim and hesitated, but one of these men pushed her into the sea. A little later she found herself wrapped in a blanket on dry soil. She never discovered who had saved her from drowning.

Évi started walking westward with a group of prisoners, looking for food. They found a dead horse, and one of the men cut it open and gave each of the group a piece of the liver. Évi didn't remember what happened after that because she collapsed into unconsciousness. The next thing she knew, she was lying in a bed between white sheets, and a nurse was asking her in German how she was feeling. Her friend Agi from the camp was in the next bed. Évi was told that she had been liberated by the British army. They had found her almost dead on the road and brought her and Agi to a hospital in Neustadt in Holstein, Germany, where she would be cared for and brought back to life. She was told that she weighed sixty-seven pounds. Then she was transferred to the DP camp where she was convalescing. It was taking her a long time to get back to her normal self.

Évi was traumatized for the rest of her life by these horrific experiences and had a lifelong fear of dogs. She was never able to testify and tell her story, anywhere, at any time, to anyone — and I never asked her about it again. But I am telling it here so that Évi's heroic act of trying to save her sisters is not forgotten, to preserve it for posterity.

After hearing this story, I was devastated because I had expected Böske to survive; she was so strong, so hopeful, such a positive thinker. My mentor, my guardian angel in Birkenau was lost to me forever except in my memories. *Thank you, thank you for saving my life, Böske.* I realized then how lucky I was in comparison with Évi. I, at least, did not have to witness the painful death of two cherished sisters.

~

In the Bergen-Belsen DP camp, in the summer of 1946, we, the three surviving siblings of the Sándor and Margit Weissenberg family, took stock of our enormous losses in the Holocaust: Our parents, Aunt Sarolta and our little nephew, Péter, and his mother, Magda Weisz, murdered in the gas chambers of Birkenau; Jenö, husband of Magda and father of Péter, and Miklós, brutally killed in Ukraine along with several cousins; Böske and Klári, starved in the Stutthof concentration camp; and a great number of aunts, uncles, cousins and second cousins and their children, whose names I no longer remember, murdered on arrival in Auschwitz-Birkenau.

Now our immediate family had shrunk to just three, and that was considered lucky in comparison to those who had survived entirely alone. From here on, we knew we were on our own and had to think seriously about our future: *How and why to go on living? What kind of life would we have? What to do next and where?*

We weren't fervent Zionists, and we were not filled with a desire to leave for what might become a Jewish homeland — not one of us. Perhaps Böske's experience there influenced us, but we did not sign up to go to British Mandate Palestine. At that time only a few survivors were let into Palestine legally by the British, and most of those who immigrated did so illegally. We heard that some of the survivors who tried to arrive in Palestine illegally were stopped by the British, who were putting survivors into some kind of refugee camp in Cyprus. We even heard that some survivors were sent back to Bergen-Belsen! Knowing this, we stayed in Bergen-Belsen until we could immigrate somewhere else. Our stay lasted about two years. I could have gone to other countries that were accepting minors, but I wouldn't be separated from my siblings. So we waited. I believe that time in Bergen-Belsen turned out to be necessary; we could start our healing and gradually transition from the concentration camps and their aftermath to the normal life we aimed for.

The Bergen-Belsen DP camp was set up in the area of Germany the British army had liberated — the British Zone as it was known. The camp had been used for German military staff and soldiers during the war. It was also near the concentration camp, which had been burned down by the liberating British military because of the typhus epidemic. The thousands of cadavers there, the people who had already died and those who died shortly after liberation, were interred in mass graves. British army officers ordered the SS soldiers they captured to carry and place the cadavers into the graves with their bare hands.

By the time Laci and I arrived there to reunite with Évi, we found a well-functioning, organized community. The British military was running the camp, but the Jewish leadership managed the daily affairs and lives of the twelve thousand people there. It was best suited to understand the needs of this nationally and religiously diverse group of traumatized Jews. The leader of the Jewish survivors, Josef Rosensaft, was president of the Central Committee of Liberated Jews in the British Zone, representing not just the DPs in Bergen-Belsen, but all Jewish DPs in the British Zone.

The camp was well managed. Food, medicine and most items needed for basic sustenance were free, supplied by the American Jewish Joint Distribution Committee (JDC) and by the Jewish Relief Unit (JRU). We even received free American cigarettes every week. Much of the staple food was obtained from American military warehouses, and all the canned stuff was khaki-coloured. We ate canned egg powder and peaches so often that I swore that after this I would never eat canned peaches again.

What was happening in Bergen-Belsen was just amazing. It was like a shtetl, a small town. People dated and fell in love, and there were many marriages in those first two years. Amazingly, bridal dresses materialized out of creative minds and golden fingers, altered from hand-me-down clothing that was donated from America. There were a few rabbis who could wed these couples. Then children were born (in that order, of course), and slowly we got used to seeing baby carriages being pushed on the streets of the camp. Life truly started to resemble something normal and, in most cases, even something happy. But we also knew that it was temporary and that one day we would have to leave this safe cocoon.

Institutions were set up. There were Yiddish schools for the children who had miraculously survived, a Yiddish newspaper called *Unzer Szytme* (Our Voice), a Yiddish theatre called *Kazet*, which means "concentration camp," and various cultural events. Everything was in Yiddish because the bulk of the Jews were from Poland, Lithuania, Romania — the remnants of Yiddish-speaking Jews. We Hungarians were a foreign species as far as the other Jews were concerned. We didn't speak Yiddish, but we learned fast. The Polish Jews were definitely in charge.

Naturally, political discussions and even heated debates became a daily pastime for most of us. We continued to be opinionated, as we had been in our past. Politically, the camp was remarkable. Jews there had strong opinions about everything, so what happened is that the adults in their twenties and thirties (there were relatively few older people who survived) and some youth groups formed according to certain ideologies — about the war, and the *Churban*, and about the emerging issue of Palestine and the possibility of an Israeli state. One might say that political parties formed in this DP camp. The Soviet Union with its Red Army was held in high esteem as one of the liberators of the camps, and socialist ideas were popular, certainly not shunned.

Our main preoccupation was with what lay ahead of us. Many survivors in Bergen-Belsen supported a self-governing Jewish presence in Palestine. So the question was Europe versus Israel. What to choose? The debate was incessant. From the supporters of Borochov on the far left to the Betar movement on the far right, and everything in between. The majority of the survivors identified with Hashomer Hatzair, a left-wing Zionist group that had been active in Central Europe before the *Churban*. The *shlichim*, the emissaries who came from the Yishuv, the Jewish community in Palestine, encouraged survivors to go there. "We're going to have an Israel. Come! Come! Come!" they would urge us with fervour. They wanted young people. They knew that the Yishuv would need fighters, and so there was a lot of propaganda to push people to make aliyah. For me these debates and discussions were new and inspiring. All this political discourse was very beneficial psychologically because we were still traumatized — even though we didn't think of ourselves that way — and it diverted our attention from our traumatic experiences and made us focus on possibilities for the future.

The Bergen-Belsen DP camp was also a place where you could always find a shoulder to cry on. We talked about our experiences all the time, at least in the Hungarian section. There were two kinds of discussions: either reminiscing about Life Before *Kazet* or about Life During *Kazet* — the horrors. Those memories were still fresh, and with us all the time.

As the days and months passed slowly, the stark reality of our temporary situation as "kept" people in a camp stared us in the face. Évi, Laci and I began thinking about our future. What next? Where to go from here with minimal life skills?

At one point, going to Brazil was a strong possibility. Our first cousin Olga Schönfeld, from Biharnagybajom, married to Miklós Klein, had managed to escape from Belgium just hours before the Nazis occupied it. We heard that good news while we were still in Debrecen, also that Miklós, who had worked in the diamond industry, had managed to take a considerable quantity of diamonds and other assets with them to Brazil. This helped them establish themselves comfortably in Rio de Janeiro and build a thriving business there too, and eventually acquire many properties. Olga didn't forget her favourite aunt, our mother, who had organized her entire wedding to Miklós in our home in Debrecen, and she managed to find us, her aunt Margitka's surviving children, in the Bergen-Belsen DP camp. She sent us affidavits, guaranteeing that they would support us, just to get us to Rio de Janeiro. And so, we hopefully waited for the day of our departure. Then the most disappointing news came, that the Brazilian government had closed its doors temporarily to new immigrants. We were told that there was a mix-up with an illegal refugee group and we wouldn't be able to get in for another five years. Our hopes to go to Brazil were dashed. Who wanted to stay in that camp and in Germany for five more years?

We waited for some other opportunities. Getting to the United States was nearly impossible. They had strict rules for letting in Jewish immigrants according to quotas that had been established based on nationality. The Hungarian quota was small and our chances of getting into the United States were not very promising. So we stayed put.

At the same time, we started to realize that no matter where we ended up, we would have to work at something to make a living. Being orphaned young, with most of our close relatives also murdered, we had little help from anyone. We could rely only on ourselves. Our young lives had been brutally interrupted, and we had little time to acquire enough education or life skills to carry us forward. It was scary. Fortunately, Évi did have sewing skills that she could rely on, and Laci started to work for the United Nations Relief and Rehabilitation Administration (UNRRA), where he gained some skills and learned a bit of English.

I was seventeen, and I too had to acquire skills. Continuing my high school education there was out of the question because of my poor knowledge of Yiddish. However, the internationally respected ORT trade school, the Organization for Rehabilitation through Training, opened a branch in our DP camp to teach and train dental technicians. An American military dental technician, Mr. Greenberg, I think his name was, an elderly man, was the teacher. The course was very popular. We learned all aspects of being a good dental technician: taking impressions, making crowns and bridges, fitting full and partial dentures and other skills. Luckily, or sadly, we had many people to learn on because many inhabitants of Bergen-Belsen had broken teeth, neglected teeth or teeth that were missing altogether. I graduated and became a full-fledged dental technician. There is a photo of me working on one of the polishing machines now hanging in the Neuberger Holocaust Education Centre in Toronto, and the original diploma is in the Bergen-Belsen Memorial Museum. Quite a few of those who took the course ended up making their living in this profession, though I was never able to use this hard-earned skill I was so proud of. But learning a trade was still important at that time; it gave me self-confidence.

As students, we also socialized, organized dances, went for long walks and formed friendships. In hindsight, my time in that DP camp was life-affirming and gave me the opportunity to slowly become a functioning human being. True, at the time we disliked it and we complained constantly. In the meantime, even with a diploma in my hands, we still had to wait for a door to open for us.

~

The Canadian government finally opened its doors to immigrants when the garment industry, in partnership with the Jewish community, launched a project, the Garment Workers Scheme, to bring over workers, who were badly needed in the garment and fur industries in Montreal, Toronto and Winnipeg. With the government's permission, Canadian Overseas Garment Commission representatives came to Bergen-Belsen to test, select and recruit a large group of us with sewing skills.

We were given to understand that being able to sew a straight seam properly was all that was needed to pass the sewing test. Laci and I practised sewing on a borrowed machine, day and night. Évi taught us, though she didn't have to practise. She was an experienced and talented seamstress, which had been helpful when she needed to obtain extra food for Klári and Böske. After liberation, when she regained her health and strength, she made her own clothing, and later she made wonderful dresses for me too, all sewn by hand as she didn't yet have access to a sewing machine.

The day of the test arrived. We had to appear before a commission of three men. We spoke Yiddish, the only common language we had. In the end, we Hungarian Jews had learned enough Yiddish to get by. Évi was the first to be tested. The men watched as she worked intently. She passed with flying colours, of course. I was next. I made the required seam. They were not sure about me, and they hesitated. We sensed a problem, and Évi told me in Hungarian that if they didn't accept me, she wouldn't go either. As the men seemed about to reject me, I said to them in my limited Yiddish, "You don't want to separate two sisters like the Germans did, do you?" I don't know where I got the courage — maybe it was utter desperation. Surprised, they looked at each other, and one of them said, "Okay, you can go too." A big sigh of relief. It worked, my daring gamble really worked.

Then it came to my brother. In spite of all the teaching and practice, Laci was silly enough to sit down at the back side of the sewing machine. His fate was sealed; they flunked him. At that time Laci was working for the UNRRA as a boy Friday, the go-to person in the organization. His advisor told Leslie — they called Laci by his English name — to let us come to Canada and that we could sponsor him to join us in three months. Indeed, that's what happened. Évi and I signed up to go to Canada.

We were so excited about leaving, but we didn't know much about Canada. It was just a country far away, and yet it was also somewhere in the world where we could work and have a chance to live a normal, peaceful life. We hoped that we had made the right choice, even though at that time Canada wasn't that welcoming to Jews. It had taken two years after the war for them to open their doors to Jewish refugees who were languishing in DP camps. For us, being part of the Garment Workers Scheme was a much-appreciated life-altering opportunity, even though this endeavour was initiated by the non-unionized section of the needle trade, something we didn't know at the time. But it wouldn't have mattered even if we knew. To leave hated, blood-soaked Europe behind and have a chance to live in Canada was all that really mattered.

Rocky Beginnings

On June 2, 1948, we sailed from Bremerhaven on a refurbished American military ship called *Ernie Pyle*, named after an American journalist and war correspondent who died in World War II. Each of us received six US dollars as pocket money. There were many displaced persons on that boat, Jews and non-Jews. Many of the women were from the Baltic countries, mainly Latvia and Estonia, and the Jews on the boat suffered from these women's antisemitic remarks. Antisemitism was the last thing we expected to accompany us on our way to a new life.

I got seasick as soon as we hit the English Channel. There was no way I could get up, never mind eat anything. The nurse insisted I drink a lot so that I wouldn't get dehydrated and somehow talked me into eating half a grapefruit. That was all I ate for three days, but I improved for the rest of the voyage. Évi was perfectly well and had a really good time in the dining room, receiving as many portions of ice cream as she wanted after dinner, as the dining room was practically empty because of mass seasickness. Eventually our ocean crossing came to an end, and we arrived in Halifax, Canada, on June 11, 1948, at the famous Pier 21, where most new immigrants landed at that time.

On our arrival at Pier 21, members of the Halifax Jewish community were waiting and greeted us with words of welcome and baskets of goodies, including foods we had not seen for years, or when it came to the bananas, ever. We were moved by this generous gesture and heartily accepted and ate their offerings. Our group of garment workers was among the first Holocaust survivors to reach Halifax, after a group of orphaned youngsters, who had been admitted to Canada before us, and the community was excited to greet us.

At the same time, not far off, the Baltic women were being greeted by nuns who were distributing holy cards with images of saints on them. The women noticed the difference in the gifts we were receiving. They were jealous and used choice words to express their hostility. We thought we had left the antisemitism behind, but we again realized that we hadn't.

From Halifax we boarded the train for Montreal. We chose Montreal only because our good friend Klára had an aunt who had settled there in the late 1930s and wanted her orphaned niece with her. This aunt was to meet Klára at the station, and when we arrived at Windsor Station, the aunt was not alone. She had brought two friends who came out of sheer curiosity to look at us DP refugees, survivors. We were a novelty, like monkeys in a cage, in a way that we did not quite comprehend. We thought we were just ordinary human beings like they were.

One of these friends, Mrs. Holzman, was from Slovakia and spoke to us in Hungarian. The women had many questions, but it was all very friendly. Mrs. Holzman took a liking to me, and suddenly she said, "Judit, I would like to adopt you." She had a young daughter, she said, but would like to help me. This took me by surprise, and I responded by telling her that my sister Évi also came with me, and I also had a brother who was still in Germany. Would she like to adopt them as well? She said that she would not, that my siblings were already adults. She was very nice though, and when she found out that we would be staying on Henri Julien Avenue, only a few doors away from her, she was so happy. From then on, Mrs. Holzman became our mentor. She and her husband and daughter, Klara, were incredibly kind to us, and we had many dinners at their table. Their friendship meant so much to us, alone in a new and strange country.

The Canadian Jewish Congress paid the first month's rent for our furnished room. They expected that we would be able to pay rent from our earnings after that. When we arrived at the flat, we could not believe we were in the New World. We faced numerous steps on a curving staircase outside the building, which we had to climb to get to the door. This was the housing style in Montreal then; every building on the street had that kind of staircase — quite treacherous during the winter months with all the snow.

The room was clean but rather dismal and uninviting. There was a double bed, a yellowing vinyl window shade and curtains, a square vinyl-topped table, two old chairs, and a chest of drawers and built-in cupboard for our clothing. The floor was covered with a dubiously coloured oilcloth, for easy washing.

We were told we would have kitchen privileges, which meant that we could cook in the kitchen, using the landlady's utensils. An older, widowed lady owned the flat and shared it with her adult daughter and son, Ida and Abe. She had another daughter who was — she wanted us to know right away — married to a rich guy. The rent was thirty dollars a month. We settled in immediately, put away our meagre belongings, took showers and went to bed. We tried to sleep but both of us ended up crying — the mattress sagged so badly. The next morning after breakfast we felt better and more positive. Crummy room or not, at least we were now in Canada!

When we had arrived in Montreal, instructions were given over the public address system at the train station in English and Yiddish. Mrs. Holzman had told us not to worry, that she was listening to all the announcements and would know exactly what we would have to do after the three days of rest. So we didn't even listen to the Yiddish announcements. We left everything up to her. We had three free days to rest or do whatever we wanted before we had to present ourselves to be assigned to our respective jobs. We used the three days to walk around the city, trying to get acquainted with the streets, laughing about some of the encounters we had that could only have happened to ignorant newcomers.

The three days of rest over, Mrs. Holzman came to tell us that we had to be assigned to our workplace. It so happened that Mrs. Holzman had *not* listened attentively to the instructions and made a big mistake. She took us to the offices of the International Ladies' Garment Workers' Union and not to the Garment Commission's office. At the union office, Mrs. Holzman told an official about our backgrounds and said that we needed jobs. The official dealing with us was very understanding and waived our initiation fee. We were then sent to a dress factory, where we started working that day. The small factory was located in an old building on Bleury Street, and again, we had to climb many stairs. It was very hot and humid that day, truly unpleasant, and it was worse indoors. We were not used to such humidity. To my utter chagrin, we were supposed to assemble complete dresses in this factory, not just sew straight seams as we had in Bergen-Belsen.

Within a few days the Garment Commission officials called Mrs. Holzman, as she had given her name as our mentor, asking her where we were and why we hadn't presented ourselves for work. She told them that she had already taken us to the union office to get work. She apologized profusely, telling them that the mistake was all hers, not to blame us. They were angry at her but did not want to start a fight with the union, and so they let the matter rest. This whole misunderstanding had an adverse impact on us. Our trip from Europe to Canada was free, paid for by the International Refugee Organization, IRO. However, the train trip from Halifax to Montreal was paid for by the Garment Commission, which was required to pay the government for every person who started working for them. Now Évi and I were excluded from this gift, and we had to pay for that trip ourselves. And so, by government order, each of us had to start repaying sixty dollars right away. Each week, one dollar was deducted from our very slim paycheque of only eight dollars a week for me and twelve for Évi. It was a tough beginning. Mrs. Holzman wanted to cover the payments, but we did not accept. We were working in a unionized factory, making a better salary.

But money was not my biggest problem. After all, we had started working, sort of. At least, Évi had started working. I was another matter. I had no dressmaking skills at all. When we received a bundle containing the pieces of the dresses, we had to assemble the parts right away, as fast as we could, into a whole dress. But I didn't recognize the pieces: which was a sleeve, a front or back, top or skirt, a collar? The forewoman spotted my predicament and my agitation right away and tried to help. While I slowly learned the basic elements of dressmaking, I was constantly nervous and despaired at my obvious inadequacy.

One day, I noticed that a liquid kept dropping onto the garment I was working on. I looked at the ceiling. Was it leaking? Then Évi, who sat right across from me, said, "Jutka, sweat is pouring down your face and will stain the dress. Wipe your face right away!" I called those beads of sweat my "sheer misery drops." I did gradually learn how to put a dress together from those puzzle pieces, but I was hopelessly slow. Speed mattered, as we did piecework and were paid for each assembled dress. The faster you worked the more money you earned. For an inexperienced person like me it was a tough grind.

We had worked at this factory for four weeks when the very apologetic boss told Évi and me that we were not producing fast enough, and as he had only twelve machines, he had to let us go. Our employer, a Jewish man who had been a factory worker during the war, had compassion. He came to tell us that he had spoken to his brother-in-law who was a foreman in a large dress factory with fifty machine operators, and he would hire us. There, it would not matter very much if two operators were slow. We were grateful and happy. Our unemployed status lasted only one day.

In our new jobs, under the tutelage of Mrs. Wallace, originally

Wallasewcky, a very kind, gentle and patient Ukrainian-Canadian forewoman, we learned to work well, and she showed us shortcuts to achieve greater speed. In time, we earned enough to make "a modest living" — a new expression for us. Naturally, I never became as good or as fast as Évi. I continued to have problems with sewing zippers into slippery velour and velvet dresses. They looked just awful. I have no idea how those dresses were ever sold.

~

We made new friends quite quickly. The secretary and bookkeeper at our first job, Gerty Goodman, befriended us. She was the second Canadian, after the Holzman family, who invited us to her home for dinner. I remember that she served a salad, which was something entirely new to us then, and calf liver. She belonged to the United Jewish People's Order (UJPO), a left-wing Jewish organization, and she drew us in as well. Sam, her husband, was a staunch socialist. They were very kind to us and helped us a lot, mainly by encouraging us when we seemed down. Sam would tell us, "Converse in English, no matter how poorly, just speak it!" At the UJPO, we made other acquaintances. We weren't anything definite politically at that point, although socialist ideas were not foreign or unwelcome to us. They had reached us via Böske and in the Bergen-Belsen DP camp. But it didn't matter. We just felt comfortable with people who genuinely took an interest in us.

In time we made other friends, too. One couple, Clare and Morris Miller, had a convertible automobile and invited us on some of their car trips, introducing us to Northern Quebec's beauty. I remember Évi and I sitting on the back seat, enjoying the wind in our hair, not realizing what the end result would be: tangled hair that looked like a couple of old mops. But the trip was fascinating. We went on a short cruise on the picturesque Saguenay River and saw interesting places like Arvida and Chicoutimi. Clare and Morris were the first friends who were truly interested in our Holocaust experiences, and they asked us many pointed questions on this trip. We had long discussions but came to the realization that there was no way to adequately explain or define even our bare existence in a camp dedicated to mass annihilation. We remained good friends for many decades.

Clare told us, "If you need to buy anything, clothing or furnishings, just tell me. I can get you anything wholesale." And that's how we bought our first new winter coats at a greatly reduced price. Morris died more than a decade ago, but I am still in touch with Clare.

In general, though, we didn't speak much about the Holocaust, especially when we noticed bizarre reactions, even from Jews. We brought the horrors right to their doorsteps, too close to ignore, and yet, there was very little interest; they simply didn't want to know. Many people weren't particularly refugee friendly either. Even those survivors who had relatives in Canada weren't always cared for very well by their relatives. The discussion about the Holocaust, when it happened, was so inane. Someone would want to know details, and a survivor would say something about acute hunger, and the response would be, "We had a tough time too. The butter was rationed during the war years." These responses were actually uttered! And so, we kept quiet and got busy with daily life, getting acquainted with our new surroundings and slowly overcoming culture shock.

In the meantime, political events were changing the world around us. With the end of the hot war came the Cold War. We Jews were always affected by the prevailing historical conditions, and so it was during the Cold War. Yesterday's (political) friends became enemies and yesterday's enemies were now friends. Communist countries started to minimize or hide what had happened to Jews in their countries during the Holocaust. The monuments they erected in memory of the victims of World War II did not specifically mention Jews. The Holocaust as a genocide, a horrendous singular historical event, was commemorated only by Yad Vashem, built in Israel in 1953. In America and Canada there were no museums yet, and the Holocaust was very distant.

With the spread of McCarthyism in the 1950s, there was heightened political repression and a campaign spreading fear of alleged Communist influence in America. Ironically, this atmosphere of fear most affected those survivors who were proud of their work in the resistance. But now they were being cautioned not to talk about their experiences so as not to be accused of being sympathetic to communism. They were now thought of as being on the wrong side of history. "Sha, shtil (Shh, hush)," these survivors were told, "or you will be accused of being a 'pinko' or a 'fellow traveller.'" So there was temporary quiet about heroism against the Nazis. The democratically elected Bundestag, the federal government in West Germany, was now America's friend, and the denazification program ended.

When, in 1960, the bombshell news hit that Eichmann had been captured in Argentina by the Mossad, Israel's intelligence agency, and would stand trial in Jerusalem and be judged by the newly created Jewish state, there was subdued jubilation among Jews, but the media condemned Israel for disregarding international law. The philandering media! How soon it forgot what the Holocaust was all about, if it ever wanted to know to begin with.

But this was a turning point. With the Eichmann trial, the entire era of the *Churban*, the great destruction, the genocide, was revealed. And as it came to the surface again, it drew the attention of the world with all its sordid, terribly disturbing and lethal details. The trial transcripts recorded the heart-wrenching stories of survivors, told in their own voices, in the language they could explain it in best, often Yiddish. Everything was still fresh. This was the start of Holocaust survivors giving public testimony, a phenomenon that later spread worldwide.

∼

Laci arrived from Germany not long after we did and came to live with us. Our landlady had a small room, really a hole in the wall, behind the kitchen, just big enough for a bed and a wardrobe and

Laci's suitcase under the bed where he kept some of his clothing. The landlady charged twenty dollars a month for this extra room, so we were now paying fifty dollars for the two rooms, a heavy financial burden for us at that point. Laci was able to find employment as a silk-screen printer.

Like most new immigrants, we had a difficult time in our adopted country in the beginning. The emotional and psychological package we came with was put on the back burner, and we focused on our ongoing life and future. Our first priority was to improve our skills so that we could make a living. Then we tried to learn the languages that allowed us to communicate properly and absorb the culture around us. Learning to decipher menus in restaurants and actually be served what we thought we ordered was a small but necessary achievement! At work we tried to manage as best we could, and there was slow but steady improvement.

To add to our difficulties, we had various conflicts with our landlady. She assumed we were ignorant and had trouble understanding that we were human beings just like her family and that we came from advanced cultures.

Thus, the first conflict started.

That summer in Montreal, Évi and I noticed that the prevailing fashion was long skirts or dresses. We wanted to look like fashionable Canadians, and so out of our very meagre earnings we managed to squeeze out five dollars for each of us to buy one summer dress. We had shorter dresses from Europe, which were good for work, but walking to work and back home (we did not have money to travel by streetcar), we wanted to look like locals. That June and July were hot and humid, a climate we were not used to, and by the time we would get home from work we would be soaking wet from perspiration. The only summer dresses we owned had to be washed, dried and ironed every day so that they would look presentable the next day. We also needed to shower every day to keep clean and refreshed. That's when all hell broke loose.

One day, when we arrived home, hot and tired, our landlady was waiting for us with a torrent of demeaning words. "You DPs," she spat the words out like dirt, "dare to shower every day when my *Canadian* children take a bath only once a week? In Auschwitz, a pail of water was good enough for you and your sisters, and in my Canadian home you're showering every day? Ha! No way!" She was yelling by the last sentence and banging the table.

Évi and I were taken aback by the tone and insulting language and started to cry. Then Évi got angry and yelled back, "We are not charity cases! We are paying you fifty dollars a month for two crummy rooms, and that's almost twice as much as your rent for the entire flat! You make a lot of money from us DPs, and that's exploitation!" Évi also pointed out that our rent included kitchen privileges and hot water usage every night. But it was no use talking sense to this elderly but rather ill-willed, stingy woman. Especially hurtful was her comparison of normal life in Montreal to Auschwitz. Did we ever regret telling her anything about our trials and tribulations in the camps! Who knew she would throw it back to us as an accusation? Later in the evening we related the whole conflict to her children, Ida and Abe, and they were more reasonable and promised to square things with their mother. Our landlady calmed down after that, but we remained uneasy in that flat and started to think about moving.

When our contract with the garment factory was coming to an end, we had to think about making other changes. I could not work as a dental technician despite the skills I learned at ORT because in Quebec at that time, one had to be a Canadian citizen to practise as a dental technician. That would take five years to happen, by which time I would have forgotten most of the required skills. But I wanted to earn a better salary than I ever could with sewing, and I imagined I would enjoy office work more. After completing the free language classes offered by the Canadian Jewish Congress, I enrolled in McGill University's part-time English extension course. My plan was to sign up for a business course when my English was good enough.

Laci decided to study accounting, and Évi was going to take a dress-designing course. By the time our contract ended, Évi, who was now a very good sample maker, got a special placement by the union. We were in no hurry, but at least we had plans.

~

Before I started a new factory job, I went on an unexpected vacation, driving with some friends to Victoria, BC. This trip, my very first vacation, was unforgettable. Except for the six-week stay in Vienna in 1946 and driving around Quebec, I had never travelled anywhere enjoyable. But now I was seeing the full beauty of Canada with all its variety of scenery, from Montreal to the flat wheat fields in Saskatchewan to the majestic and breathtaking Rocky Mountains. We entered the Rockies at Pocahontas, Jasper National Park. Driving south through the mountains toward the Columbia Icefield, then Lake Louise and Banff, I was treated to additional glorious landscapes and was awed. I didn't miss the factory and dressmaking one iota; instead I gained a new respect for Canada's size and natural grandeur.

Returning from this wonderful vacation, I found a job in another dress factory, Kerner Dress Co., as a piecework operator, like before. By that time, I was considered experienced and I had a good command of English and also some ability to converse in French. I was also well-acquainted with the method of payment. A price committee of three people, chosen from the ranks of the factory's dress operators, would examine a new garment, assess how long it would take to sew one, and based on that how many dresses could be produced in an eight-hour workday. They would then establish how much money an operator would make in a day. Naturally, complicated and fussy dresses take longer to make, and the price-per-piece had to be set accordingly so that we could make a decent living while working on those garments. After consulting with the rest of the workers, the committee would present the employer with a price-per-garment. The employer would of course start bargaining with the committee and offer much less. This was called the confrontational bargaining approach. If all went well, with haggling and compromises on each side, we would eventually come to an agreement, and the dress would go into production. Every new garment went through this process, which was tedious but necessary. If the committee and the boss could not agree on a price, a union representative was summoned to negotiate. Officially, the union rep was supposed to represent the workers' interest, but that was often not the case.

I am not exactly sure how or why I was chosen as the third member of the price committee at Kerner Dress Co. Perhaps it was because my English and French were good and I was an outspoken, fearless workers' advocate, certainly not because I was an excellent dress operator. The other two committee members were French-Canadian.

It happened one day that the boss showed us a very fancy, complicated sample dress that had been brought in from New York. He had obtained a large order for it from Simpson's department store. I can't remember now how much we asked per piece with that dress, but I recall that there was a seventy-five-cent difference between our asking price and the boss's offer. That was a huge difference. We couldn't come to terms, so the boss called in the union rep, who thought we were really backward. He was trying to be conciliatory and said, "Girls, girls" — we were always just "girls" — and then suggested that we start sewing the dresses and then come to terms. We were shocked. Once we started making the dress, we would never win the price we needed. No! All three of us agreed that we would not start sewing without agreeing on a price. We haggled back and forth some more, but we couldn't come even close to the price we wanted.

We presented Mr. Kerner's final offer to forty dress operators and they, in unison, said, "No. Either we get the amount we need or we don't sew." But the boss was adamant and would not change his final offer. So, the three of us on the price committee walked right back to the factory and simply turned off the power to all the machines. We went on what was called a wildcat strike, without the support of the union rep. After all, it was *our* livelihood that was at stake. We would not start working. Mr. Kerner came to the factory to talk to us. He pointed to me and told me to come back to the office.

"Tell me," he said, "what is a nice Jewish girl like you doing on the price committee?"

I said, "Mr. Kerner, this nice Jewish girl also has to make a living, and with what you are offering, none of us can."

Finally, the union rep came back and we settled for fifteen cents less than we had asked for. It was a rewarding fight. The dress went into production immediately. I am sure that both Mr. Kerner and Simpson's made a handsome profit, and we "girls" made decent salaries to boot.

I don't know how all this came about. I was in such a weak position, with no parents and no rich, powerful people behind me — only my equally poor but loyal siblings. My job was very important, but something told me that there was also social justice. Maybe my Hashomer Hatzair sister, Böske, beckoned? As it happened, this would be the last dress factory I worked in.

There was another moment not long after when this same kind of strange mixture of foolish and desperate courage took hold of me. After I finished my business course, when I was twenty-two, I had to look for an office job that would pay enough so that I wouldn't be a burden to Évi or Laci. I said goodbye to all my co-workers at Kerner Dress Co., wished them continued well-being, and in turn they hugged me and wished me a better future.

But it wasn't easy to find an office job without at least two years of Canadian experience. Plus, though my typing was immaculately accurate, it proved to be too slow. I wondered why everybody was in such a hurry and needed speed typists. After six weeks of job searching and interviewing, I saw a tiny advertisement in the *Adler*, a Montreal Jewish newspaper: "Seeking assistant bookkeeper with typing ability for a textile wholesale company's office. Ask for Mr. Sam Macklin."

The next morning, I was at the address, the small newspaper ad in my hand, and was greeted by Mr. Macklin junior, the son, pipe in his mouth and dark-rimmed glasses on top of his head. After I introduced myself, he indicated to Jack, the bookkeeper, to get a desk ready, and I understood immediately that he wanted to test my typing. I really wanted to get this job, and once again I gambled. I said, "Mr. Macklin, if you have in mind to test my typing, I am leaving." He pushed his glasses to the tip of his nose, looked at me curiously and asked, "Why?" I told him that I got nervous when my typing was watched and couldn't perform properly. He smiled and said, "You're hired." Just like that. I was stunned and extremely happy. I was to be Jack's assistant and start the next morning. It was the beginning of an entirely new phase of my life in Canada, and I gladly waved goodbye to piecework.

Jack proved to be a real mensch and a very patient and thorough teacher, and I learned quickly. Much of the typing I had to do was for Mr. Macklin junior, who was involved with building a new curling club for Jews in Montreal because the existing one did not allow Jews to join. With my background, that was very disturbing news for me. In Canada too, I asked?

~

On the home front, we finally moved. Laci found us a flat on a busy street, Saint Laurent Boulevard, in the home of a non-Jewish Hungarian couple, Mr. and Mrs. Söreg. They had a huge apartment with many rooms, and we rented two very nice rooms for forty-five dollars with all privileges. We were treated with respect and kindness, and Mrs. Söreg often served us lovely dinners, cooked with real Hungarian flavour. She was a good cook and a very decent lady.

Évi and I witnessed a frightening scene while living in this flat, another slice of history. One weekend morning in 1952, we became aware of a loud, unfamiliar noise coming from the street. From our windows we saw a large crowd of young women demonstrating. They were workers on strike against the French-Canadian department store, Dupuis Frères. The strike was loud but peaceful. We watched as police on horseback rushed into the crowd of women indiscriminately to disperse them. Several of the women were injured, and many of them were crying and shouting in anger at the police. With our Holocaust memories, Évi and I were simply shocked and terrified to see something like this happening in Montreal. Police brutality was permitted in Canada too?

We were at the Söreg's apartment for a couple of years and then moved a few times. One move was to Outremont, a welcome upgrade to a very nice district and a beautiful apartment we shared with our friends Dora and Otto Smilowics and their young son. The expansion of the Smilowics family necessitated our next move. Évi and I found a place of our own in the Park Extension district, a newly developed working-class neighbourhood, where the two of us could easily afford to rent a lovely apartment in a new building — all modern, sparkling and clean. Financially, we were much better off now. Évi had graduated with a diploma in dress designing but was afraid to leave the security she had as a sample maker. But she made good money and stayed with sample making until she retired at age sixty-one. Laci, who now went by Leslie, had finished his accounting courses and moved to Toronto, where most of his friends from Bergen-Belsen had settled down and he thought it would be easier to find work. A couple of years later he married and moved to Detroit, where he worked as a controller for twenty years.

At this point, I was no longer working for Mr. Macklin, though we had parted in a most cordial way. I had received a better offer from three friends who had started a real estate business, Concordia Estates Limited. The company was managing several mid-size apartment buildings for absentee owners. Not only was the pay double, I was attracted to the challenge of learning different skills and having new experiences. I didn't know it then, but this would be my last job in Montreal.

In this new position, I maintained the accounting books and dealt with the service people and tenants, eventually becoming an assistant property manager. Being multilingual came in handy as I was the main contact for tenants, many of whom were immigrants. I remember once typing a letter while one of my bosses was standing behind me. When I finished, he asked if he could see the letter. Surprised, I handed it to him. "You were typing in English but conversing with a tenant on the phone in Yiddish. How do you do that?" "Sheer talent," I said jokingly.

It was tricky to work for friends, but with mutual respect (and lots of humour) it worked out well. Humans, I realized in this job, were unpredictable in the variety of their demands. I learned to expect the unexpected, and to deal with it, mostly successfully. Though I must confess, I never became a speed typist.

To Love and Be Loved

My life was humming along happily enough. Then, one day in 1959, I received a phone call from a man named Sidney Cohen. He brought me greetings from a mutual friend with whom he worked in his office in Toronto and said that I came "highly recommended" to have a date with. He was in Montreal on a new business assignment and would I meet him? He sounded rather pleasant on the phone, and on a whim I said yes.

Without realizing it, I suggested an expensive restaurant, and Sidney and I spent a most enjoyable dinner, with wine and all the trimmings, conversing the whole time. I remember that the dinner cost twenty-five dollars, a lot of money in those days. The story of this expensive dinner date would become a family legend, and I would be referred to jokingly as "the gold-digger date."

Sidney and I parted amicably, and he asked if he could call me again. I said yes. His new assignment would bring him to Montreal for one week a month until the project was finished. Sidney was working for Southam Business Publications as a market researcher and sales rep. He had a diploma in radio broadcasting and wanted to study further, but his widowed mother could not afford to help him get a higher education. He had initially looked for employment in the advertising business, but at that time, people with names like Cohen were not welcome in that industry.

Our relationship deepened. I invited Sidney to our home, where he met Évi and could enjoy her cooking, especially her soups. He told us that he had grown up during the depression years on bread and soups. "Évi's soups are excellent!" Sid declared, and Évi beamed. Ours turned out to be a long-distance courtship, and I travelled to Toronto to meet and get to know his widowed mother, Sarey, and his brother and sister-in-law, Leon and Adele, and their young daughter, Kathi.

Sidney Jessel Cohen and I married one and a half years after we met, on June 9, 1961, in Montreal in a rabbi's study with two witnesses from the family. The ceremony was followed by a dinner with eight close friends and then a modest wedding party at the Capri Hotel, where we danced with joy. There were fifty young friends and very few elderly people (except for our old friends, the Vertes family — Marci, Lili, Gabi and Agi — recently arrived from Hungary). This was typical of Holocaust survivors' weddings in those days. In addition to creating my beautiful three-piece wedding outfit, Évi covered the cost of the drinks as a wedding gift, and the late Sam Balderman, who along with his wife, Yvonne, were close friends, played dance music with his small band as his gift to us. Sid's mom, my late and beloved mother-in-law, organized a beautiful party in her home in Toronto for the Jessel and Cohen families. The arrangements were perfect. We were happy.

For our honeymoon, we drove east, through New England and the Maritime provinces, ending up in Glace Bay, Nova Scotia, the birthplace of Sid's father and where all his Cohen uncles, aunts and cousins had grown up. A few of them still lived there, and I met Sid's very elderly Cohen grandmother. I, who had lost most of my extended family and much of my immediate family in the Holocaust, was rather appreciative of Sid's family. Our honeymoon introduced me to another part of Canada and was filled with new discoveries. It was a sweet, romantic, unique and meaningful trip.

Back in Toronto, we started our married life living with Sarey, in her home in the Bathurst Manor neighbourhood. Later, Sarey moved into a lovely newly decorated bachelor suite, and Sid and I rented an apartment a few blocks from where she lived so that we could be in close contact with her at all times.

It took me some years to get used to living in Toronto. It was so different from my beloved, vibrant, exciting Montreal that I had come to cherish. I missed Évi and felt guilty about leaving her alone in Montreal, in spite of knowing that she had a circle of close friends. I tried to persuade her to move to Toronto, but she said that she had all her friends there. Not only that, visiting me would be a nice change for her. This became particularly true when we had children. Évi adored them, and they reciprocated with hugs and kisses. When she visited when they were older, they would step into the house after school and start yelling joyfully, "Auntie Éva is here!" They could smell the mouth-watering aromas from her baking and cooking wafting through the house. Évi was always included in our travels abroad and came along whenever she felt like it.

Moving to Toronto, I also left behind a number of long-time friends like Dinah and Abe Shuster and Andy and Maggie Taussig and their children, with whom I had forged strong ties. (I was the maid of honour at Dinah Shuster's wedding. She passed away recently, and I lost a very dear friend.) With them, and others, I had shared left-wing ideas and political activities at the UJPO. These activities had stopped in 1956, shortly after the truth about the Stalinist regime's brutality became known to the world, but our friendships endured. I am still in touch with a few of these friends today, sixty years later. Also enduring is my strong belief in the need for social and economic justice in our society; social democracy is still my favourite ideology.

As Sid and I built our new life in Toronto, our priorities became clear. Having such a small immediate family, I wanted to develop closer relationships with my in-laws, especially after we had children. We made a point of getting together with Leon and Adele and their daughters, Kathi and later, Natalie, on major Jewish holidays and sometimes on birthdays or for casual visits. The kids loved the celebrations, and we wanted to pass on the traditions. Sadly, both Leon and Adele passed away a few years ago.

I also wanted to get back to work. This may sound strange, but in Toronto at that time, nobody wanted to hire a female assistant property manager, even one with bookkeeping knowledge. I learned to drive, thinking this might make finding a job easier. In the end, I settled for working as a bookkeeper only, occasionally helping the co-owner of a large apartment building with management duties. I left this job eventually to find something closer to where I lived, doing similar work on a smaller scale for two very pleasant elderly Jewish gentlemen, one of them a Holocaust survivor and by then pretty well-to-do. With amusement, I recall how they tried to convince me to buy shares in Xerox, predicting a very handsome return eventually. Were they ever correct! But for us, borrowing that kind of money — two thousand dollars to invest— was out of reach.

I left this job two weeks before I gave birth to our daughter, Michelle Elizabeth, in 1964. We named her after my late, beloved mother, Margit, and my sister Böske, Elizabeth in English. With time, I learned to love and be loved again and had the courage to grow branches on my shattered family tree. Four years after Michelle's birth, we adopted our son, Jonathan Alexander, who was named after Sid's father and my father, Sándor. I stayed at home for twelve years, enjoying raising the children with a lot of help from Sid. He was always a most loving, considerate husband and father, enchanting all of us every Valentine's Day with funny and loving hand-drawn greetings pinned on our bedroom doors — an everlasting memory of childhood for Michelle and Jonathan. He also understood my needs. He never shied away from washing the kitchen floor when I was pregnant or from cooking dinners. My mother-in-law had told me at the very beginning, "You'll see, Judy, he will be a very good husband because he was always a very good and helpful son." Sarey had been widowed at thirty, when her husband, Nathan, died of a rare type of leukemia at the age of thirty-eight. Leon was twelve and Sid ten. Tragically, Sarey died of lung cancer at the age of fifty-nine — so young! Michelle was six and Jonathan two when she died, and our children missed out on having the only grandparent they had known accompany them to their adulthood. It would have been an important relationship for them emotionally.

My main activities after the children started school were connected to their development: I dealt with the schools and their studies, their teachers, extracurricular activities and other educational matters. The idea of multiculturalism was just starting to emerge in our predominantly Anglo-Saxon culture and in schools, with students coming from varied ethnic and cultural backgrounds. I watched closely, as my children were part of that trend. I also became part of a group of women that was lobbying for French immersion programs in public schools. Looking to the future, I thought that being bilingual in Canada would have advantages. Plus, learning two languages is good for brain development — so we were told by the experts. I, who had been exposed to two foreign languages from first grade on, knew from experience how helpful it could be to master as many languages as possible. Finally, a program was established in our school district when Jonathan had just reached the age for enrollment. Michelle, almost four years older, missed out on it.

Satisfying as all that was, at one point I started to crave activities that would enhance my leisure time. So I enrolled in a university extension course and studied cultural anthropology. After that, at the urging of my friend Honey Ross, we both enrolled at the Ontario College of Art (now called the Ontario College of Art and Design, or OCAD) to study pottery. Kneading the rich, dark clay was a remarkable way to relieve the frustrations we encountered at home. And I found great satisfaction in learning to create hand-built items, using my imagination and newly learned skills. I pursued this for a good number of years, and I still have a few pieces to remind me of this creative period in my life. At another studio, I learned to do raku pottery, using a Japanese firing process, which eventually became my favourite endeavour.

As a family, we tried to have fun times too, and at one stage, camping seemed to be the way to do it. During long car rides, Jonathan, who was an accomplished reader by age four, would happily keep occupied with a dozen books. Michelle would stay busy with her Barbie dolls or would nap. On these trips, we met congenial and interesting people. Campers are a special breed, aware and appreciative of nature in the raw, and mindful of taking good care of it. Sid was one of these people and inculcated the same reverence for nature in the children. Michelle especially became a nature lover like Sid.

Often we would meet up with some of our friends from Montreal on these camping trips. These were truly grand times — exploring new terrain, in the USA and Canada, in inclement or pleasant weather conditions, and ending our days with sumptuous dinners in the evenings. Our friends' older daughter, Sharon Shuster, a young teenager then, would play the guitar, and we would all sing folk songs we knew so well and drink Andy Taussig's excellent wine.

Our camping trips ended when the children got older and we bought a cottage on Galla Lake. Winter was a favourite time to go up north. The terrain was covered in pristine white snow, not like in the city, and trees glistened with frozen water drops. It was magical and delighted the children. In autumn, the grounds were covered with incredibly colourful leaves, like a beautifully woven carpet. In summer, the lake was the attraction. Sid and Michelle loved to canoe on the lake and listen to the loons in the early morning when it was quiet. Jonathan and I often went raspberry picking, covered in netted hats for protection from mosquitoes. Friends would come up to visit and stay overnight for a few poker games.

Looking back, this was an easy, enjoyable phase in our lives, even with the occasional bickering that was inevitable as the kids asserted themselves more and more. This time, too, came to an end when the children no longer wished to spend their weekends away from their friends in the city but were too young to be left at home on their own. We sold the cottage and used the money to move to an area of the city where our children wanted to go to school.

When we moved, we also joined Temple Emanu-El, a Reform congregation. Jonathan enjoyed their youth group and summer camp, and Sid and I made new friends in the congregation. I loved the liturgical music of the services ever since I was a young girl in Debrecen, and I was always interested in current social and political issues and had ample opportunity to become active on the Social Action, Adult Education and Israel committees.

When Jonathan turned thirteen, in 1981, we decided to have his bar mitzvah in Israel at the Kotel, the Western Wall. Évi and Leslie joined us, and it was an unforgettable experience. We visited Moshav Neviot on the banks of the Red Sea, south of Eilat, an area that was then under the control of Israel. While the braver family members went on camel rides, I toured a large part of the Sinai Peninsula, and at one point our group was hosted by a Bedouin shepherd and his grandson who served us the most delicious spiced tea. These are cherished memories, both because of the personal experiences we had and because we were witnessing the revival of our Jewish peoplehood and the incredible progress Israel was making as a country. Sadly, the much-desired peace with her Palestinian neighbours is not a reality just yet.

~

Life wasn't always smooth sailing. In 1989, our first post-Holocaust tragedy struck. My dearly beloved sister Évi died after a relatively short illness — complications arising from skin cancer, a blood transfusion gone terribly wrong. She was the first death Leslie and I had to deal with after the Holocaust. Losing her was extremely painful and still is. I have never stopped missing her and never will. Five years after Évi's death, Leslie, my last living sibling, died of lung cancer.

There was nobody left for me to reminisce and laugh with about our childhood shenanigans — a void nothing can fill.

As a Holocaust survivor, I broached my personal story with my children when it was age-appropriate — first during a Passover dinner, connecting the topics of slavery and freedom to what happened to me as a young teenager, explaining why they didn't have grandparents from my side and trying to satisfy their frequent questions. I tried not to traumatize them with horror stories. I didn't want them to fear being Jewish.

Child-rearing is a delicate and complicated endeavour, and parents are never quite ready for it. As the saying goes, "little kids, little problems — big kids, big problems," and I found the young-adult phase difficult to handle. I was always worried about drugs. This was after LSD was popularized in the 1960s by Harvard psychologist Timothy Leary, which, as we were told, produced vivid hallucinations. The 1960s and '70s produced an entire counterculture of drug abuse that I constantly dreaded. Somehow my acculturation didn't cover this. The youth culture was changing, and rough, vulgar, disrespectful language entered mainstream communication and was acquired from school buddies and other influences.

I often clashed with Michelle, and this was a frustrating time for me. I was still very much a European and remembered the way I was brought up. But Sid, a second-generation Canadian, took this in stride and would try to calm me down. There was a culture clash in my own family! I didn't seem to have the right tools to analyze, comprehend and compromise. Much later, when Michelle was around twenty, she said something very profound: "You know why you couldn't handle me when I was a defiant teenager? Because by the time *you* reached sixteen, you had no parents to rebel against." Indeed, my sweet-sixteen was spent in the shadow of the gas chambers, where my parents had been murdered a few months earlier, without even graves where I could place little memory stones.

Jonathan was a calm and pliable individual who disliked arguments of all kinds. At age seventeen, he came out and told us that he was gay. While at home we fully supported him with love and understanding, like most young gay people at that time, he suffered from discrimination and exclusion by his peers. However, Michelle, then a college student who had a summer job in social work, helped him to find a group where he could get counselling, and slowly his emotional equilibrium and self-confidence was strengthened.

The time eventually came when I felt the need to ease back into work, and I ended up working in a public relations company's accounting department four days a week for eleven years. It was good for me. I met people much younger than I was — hard workers who were vibrant, intelligent and funny. Most believed implicitly in the value of their work, and their zest for life and fun was catchy. I also met people from different backgrounds: Michi, a young Japanese-Canadian woman and Judy Lem, a Chinese-Canadian woman. With these friendships, my horizons expanded and my social world was enriched. Judy would tell me about Chinese customs and her parents' difficult and dangerous wartime experiences in mainland China. She in turn learned about my Holocaust horror stories. We learned from each other how widespread the hate, destruction and suffering was during the World War II era, both in the Far East and in Europe. Judy and I are still in touch, sending each other greetings on birthdays.

In addition to my work, I volunteered with Alzheimer's patients at the Baycrest Centre for Geriatric Care. Dealing with these patients, even in the earlier stages of their illness, was heartbreaking, but it was uplifting when I felt I made a difference. I still spoke Hungarian well, and I was able to converse with some of the patients who, because of their Alzheimer's, reverted to their native Hungarian.

With the passing of time, our children became adults and attended to their university studies and their futures. Michelle grew into a lovely, enterprising and intelligent young woman who was actively involved in social issues, which pleased me. Economic justice and gender equality were her major concerns, and she ended up interrupting her doctoral studies to work for a major Canadian trade union. Politically we were on the same page, and I learned a great deal from her. She later supported my efforts to create a website on the issue of women in the Holocaust, a theme she had written about in her master's thesis. But there was always tension between us. And I sometimes wonder if it is because I am, or am considered, a "damaged" Holocaust survivor.

Jonathan, always a good student, sailed through the French immersion stream and eventually got two degrees, including a law degree, and began to work as a technical and promotional writer. He also has a published book under his belt. To this day, we have a loving and mutually respectful relationship, and he often calms me down when I get unduly irritated by what he calls inconsequential issues.

Sidney worked at Southam for thirty years and then at Key Media, where he developed a magazine called *Where*, a travel guide that was used internationally. He had a stellar reputation in the Canadian Business Press and won several awards. Those were the times when one could achieve advancement, recognition and success through sheer hard work, ambition, a good dose of intelligence, producing innovative ideas and offering loyalty to a company — without any university degrees. Sid was with Key Media for seventeen years, until he retired.

When I finally reached the age when company policy dictated that I had to retire, I was ready. I received the usual gift, the customary party and said goodbye to PR work and to my delightful co-workers, just as at one time, way back when, I said goodbye to the price-committee members in a dress factory in Montreal. It was my sixty-fifth birthday, September 17, 1993.

Activist Years

On a sunny May afternoon, a few months before I retired, I was taking my lunch-hour stroll in the streets of downtown Toronto when I became aware of a noise coming from nearby. I turned the corner off Bloor and headed north on Bay Street to try to see what the shouting was about, and I saw a group of young people clad in black leather and walking in a circle carrying placards and shouting the slogan "White Power! White Power!" I had an automatic reaction — a fear, like my clenched stomach in Birkenau during selections — a certain kind of nauseating, extreme fear that returned unbeckoned. And for a terrifying few seconds, the lines were blurred between past and present. I wondered, was I looking back at history or ahead? I approached the crowd, and suddenly I was face-to-face with a group I had heard and read about, but never met in the flesh. It was the Heritage Front, a group of white-supremacist, neo-Nazi Holocaust deniers.

My shock at this vision subsided quickly, but my anger did not. I decided to do something — anything. I approached the group. The leader, a man I later learned was Wolfgang Dröge, stood in front of the meagre, spontaneous gathering of pedestrians and spoke. What I caught was this: "You know there was no such thing as black slavery in the United States...." I thought that next he was going to say that there was no such thing as the Holocaust, but he didn't have a chance to utter anything more because I stepped right between him and the little audience. Angry and agitated, I spoke to these curiosity seekers.

"Don't listen to him," I said. "He is nothing but a bloody neo-Nazi! And they would like to repeat what the Nazis did in Europe fifty years ago."

Dröge just looked at me, surprised. Maybe it was my accent, but he must have figured he was not going to argue with me. He walked away and rejoined the group. I admit I wasn't such a hero because there were four police officers watching the scene. One of them sensed how upset I was and came over to me and said, "Lady, don't aggravate yourself. They only have a permit for twenty minutes, and then they have to disperse." My luck! I caught the twenty minutes that would soon spur me to action.

The group did disperse, after yelling "White power!" many more times. I went up to the one young woman I noticed in the group and asked her, "What are you doing with such scum?" She looked at me and shrugged her shoulders. The image of her walking away has stayed with me to this day.

I walked back to the office very disheartened and then left for the day, too aggravated to do any work. Nazism, irrational hatred as we knew it in Europe, was dormant for a while only; it was still alive and well, and now dwelling in my adopted city.

Four months later, two days after I retired, I visited the Toronto Holocaust Centre (now the Neuberger Holocaust Education Centre). I wanted to find out how I could get involved in fighting back against this emerging assault on the Holocaust and historical truth. It was the first time in my adult life that I was able to luxuriate in total freedom, but this work could not be postponed. At the Holocaust Centre, I asked the then-director, Peninah Zilberman, what I as a survivor could do to combat Holocaust denial. She said, "Start telling your story. Learn by listening and observing others who have been doing it for a while." I wasn't sure I could tell my story, but I had to try. I was encouraged by my good friend, the late Stephen Bleyer, who miraculously survived alone in Auschwitz-Birkenau until he was liberated by the Soviet army in January 1945. He was fourteen years old and severely emaciated. In time, he became well-known in Montreal as a public speaker who lectured about the Holocaust and combatting racism. He also became the president of the Montreal Holocaust Memorial Centre (now the Montreal Holocaust Museum). His speeches taught me a lot about the relevant and important issues to emphasize when I told my own story.

And so, I was catapulted into an endeavour I could never have envisaged for my last phase of life, making these years incredibly meaningful, though I am slowing down now. I became a frequent speaker in high schools and universities across Canada and in a few universities in the United States. As an activist and public speaker at the Toronto Holocaust Centre for twenty-seven years, I was also the co-chair of the speakers' bureau for a good number of years, and I got to know many of our survivor speakers as friends, supporting them in becoming effective public speakers. This involvement eventually led me to seek a way to permanently honour our speakers, who devoted so much of their time and energies to educating hundreds of young students about the Holocaust. And so, I initiated and chaired the permanent exhibit *We Who Survived*, a photographic tribute to our speakers. On opening night of the exhibit, I received my real reward: About a dozen survivors who were part of the exhibit came to me to express their deep appreciation for initiating this project while they were still living and able to experience it with their families. I also participated in four March of the Living missions as a survivor-facilitator for student groups.

I have spoken to many hundreds of students and adults, trying very hard to make my young and not-so-young audiences understand that they need to know about this unprecedented, civilization-shattering genocide for their own sakes — to be historically knowledgeable, and to be able to recognize the signs if and when something similar re-emerges, and combat it. I have urged the students not to cry about my sad story but to *think* about the important issues I raised. That was and is my goal.

What Women?

As I embarked on learning about public speaking and began to talk about my own experiences in the Holocaust, I became interested in expanding my knowledge of what had happened beyond the personal. The nagging question came to haunt me time and again: How could the Holocaust, in all its enormity, as well as in its minute details, have happened? How and why? Six million Jews, hundreds of thousands of Roma and many others, murdered mercilessly by people who were supposedly cultured and educated.

By this time, there were many resources on the history of the Holocaust, as well as memoirs and diaries. I started reading: Raul Hilberg's *The Destruction of the European Jews*; Emanuel Ringelblum's *Notes from the Warsaw Ghetto*; Christopher Browning's *Ordinary Men: Reserve Police Battalion 101 and the Final Solution in Poland*, just to name a few. And then there were the widely read memoirs, Primo Levi's *Survival in Auschwitz* and Elie Wiesel's *Night*. Diaries, the mute testimonies left behind by those who were murdered, along with the collective voices of survivors and their written memoirs, are still helping historians and social scientists understand the details of what happened.

But as the stories came out, it seemed to me that the entire narrative of the Holocaust was seen through the eyes of men, that it was, in the words written by Professor John K. Roth, an "ungendered unity of experience." As more memoirs and testimonies by female survivors appeared in English — starting with Anne Frank's *The Diary of a Young Girl* (1952); and then Isabella Leitner's *Fragments of Isabella: A Memoir of Auschwitz* (1978); Etty Hillesum's *An Interrupted Life: The Diaries and Letters of Etty Hillesum* (1983); Lucille Eichengreen's *From Ashes to Life: My Memories of the Holocaust* (1994); Olga Lengyel's *Five Chimneys* (1995); and hundreds more — scholars began to hear other voices and paid attention to them.

In 1983, Drs. Joan Ringelheim and Esther Katz convened a conference called "Women Surviving: The Holocaust," the first of its kind. I managed to obtain a copy of the proceedings, which outlined the aim of the conference, to open up a new era of research on women and put the issue of gender on the Holocaust-studies map.

Then, one Mother's Day, my daughter, who was enrolled in a women's studies program, surprised me with a book, *Different Voices: Women and the Holocaust,* edited by Drs. John K. Roth and Carol Rittner, two non-Jewish, noted scholars in the United States. I was blown away by the writings of the scholars and survivors in this book, which is still a classic. I continued to read and educate myself about women's roles in the ghettos and in the armed and unarmed resistance. I also learned about the immense suffering of women and their struggles to survive in the places I knew so intimately myself.

It is clear that every Jewish woman, man and child was equally targeted for total annihilation as Jews, first and foremost. And yet, exploring gender differences can, according to scholars, deepen our understanding of these events that defy comprehension. This does not mean competing for a place in a hierarchy of suffering. On the contrary, the aim of researching gender-specific suffering in the Holocaust is to hear the voices of *all* the victims — those who survived and those who did not — so as to enhance our understanding of history. Scholars agree that the voices and writings of women survivors comprise a unique genre, one that is driven by the twin circumstances of racism and biology, revealing women's double vulnerability — first as Jews and second as women. As Dr. Esther Fuchs states in her book, *Women and the Holocaust: Narrative and Representation*, "By ignoring gender, we stand to miss one of the most lethal weapons of Nazi propaganda and persecution…. Antisemitism and misogyny were interconnected in the Nazi apparatus." I could easily agree with this premise, as I had felt the effects of both.

With my new internet skills, for which I am forever indebted to my son, Jonathan, I began to read online as well, and I found at least one pretty extensive Holocaust website, remember.org. I emailed the editor, and after I praised the content, I asked, "And where are the women on your website?" I soon received a reply in the form of a question: "What women?"

This was another pivotal point in my life. In 2001, I decided that in addition to my public speaking engagements, teaching about the genocide of approximately half a million Hungarian Jews through my personal experiences within their historical context, I would have an additional task. I felt compelled to create a website dedicated to the women of the Holocaust, chronicling the horrors they experienced because of their Jewishness, as well as the added layer of gender and sex-related abuse that characterized the struggles of women to survive under the Nazi yoke. I also felt drawn to this work by my memory of the Kanada *Kommando* when we arrived in Birkenau, their urging, "Give the children to the grandmothers" in an attempt to save the young mothers.

I was of the opinion that academia must not talk only to academia, that all the significant papers, research materials and knowledge about women in the Holocaust must get to a much wider audience, especially to students in universities and high schools. I was determined. And so, with a friend's technical help and my editorial work, the site Women and the Holocaust — a Cyberspace of Their Own was created. The acknowledgement page credits everyone who has graciously and generously helped, in different capacities, including my dear husband Sid, who endured, with Job-like patience, the long hours I spent at the computer.

I wanted to fill the site with educational material that would be a bridge between academia and the internet-using public at large. I tried to construct something worthwhile that might become a good teaching tool on a topic that suffered from a paucity of public exposure. I hoped also that at least a few members of the next generation working in higher education would not just be interested in reading the material on the website but would be inspired to study and research it further, and one day teach it. One such brilliant undergraduate student who told me that I influenced him was Tomaz Jardim at Trent University. He became a friend and a noted professor at Ryerson University.

To begin with, I wanted to record survivors' stories. I approached several survivors through the Neuberger Holocaust Centre, and I transcribed and published their stories under "Personal Reflections." This was rewarding but very time-consuming, and eventually I asked survivors to give me written stories to publish. I received many stories, including a number from Hungary that had been translated into English. Little by little, the number of stories grew.

Getting material from scholars was another challenge. At that point, being published on the internet was not considered prestigious. But I had my own vision, and it proved to be correct. I had the good fortune to meet the late Dr. Yaffa Eliach, with whom I became friends. She was a pioneer in the field of Holocaust research and the founder of New York's Center for Holocaust Studies, which had published a newsletter about women partisan fighters and resistance workers in 1990. I asked her if I could publish some of those stories on my website. Yaffa looked at me with a big smile. "Judy, you can have the entire issue, publish them all." I published the stories under the heading "Women of Valour." This was the best possible encouragement I could have received.

Next, I approached Dr. Myrna Goldenberg, the noted Holocaust scholar who coined the famous expression "different horrors, same hell" to describe women's suffering in Nazi captivity. She became one of my friends and major supporters and was generous with her encouragement and contributions. Her essays were also published on my website. A dear friend, Dr. Karin Doerr, undertook the monumental work of creating the many-faceted bibliography and updating it, and her husband, Dr. Gary Evans, curates the filmography section. A number of other scholars — Dr. Joan Simalchik, Dr. Sara Horowitz, Dr. Dalia Ofer, and Drs. Rochelle Saidel and Sonja Hedgepeth, who have written extensively on Jewish women's sexual abuse in Ravensbrück and in other camps — either contributed or were supportive of my website and its raison d'être. In an essay in the book *Experience and Expression: Women, the Nazis, and the Holocaust*, Professor John K. Roth acknowledges my vision in using the internet for Holocaust education, specifically to talk about the issue of gender, and has kind words to say about my website.

My website also contains book reviews, poetry, short stories, stories that children and grandchildren of survivors have contributed, stories about motherhood, early testimonies by women given to the Central Jewish Historical Commission in Warsaw in 1944–1945, and stories of reflection written by survivors years after the liberation. I am indebted to so many people who, along with me, saw the important mandate of this still-timely website. I am glad I had the strength to do it. After all, it is a tribute to half the Jewish people who experienced the Holocaust.

Sadly, in Canada, the academic and Holocaust-education community in general has been very slow to promote greater awareness of women's experiences in the Holocaust — both in terms of what was done to them and how they coped with the horrors of survival. However, there have been positive developments in general, and a good number of conferences, books and exhibits have been created. In 2007, Yad Vashem created an international exhibit, *Spots of Light: To Be a Woman in the Holocaust*, and in 2018, they turned it into an online exhibit, acknowledging that "women, men and children followed different paths to death."

Facing New Challenges

As the years roll by, I observe how history continues to change around us. Some of those changes are imperceptible at first, but they have sped up with the advent of social media platforms such as Facebook, Twitter and Instagram. Many people hoped that these platforms would carry the promise of "never again" that developed when we still believed that the vision of peace and harmony laid out by the United Nations could be realized. I am often chagrined by what I see.

The Holocaust and its impact, no matter how widely taught, doesn't seem to be a deterrent, and it was followed by genocides that morphed "never again" into "again, and yet again": the Rwandan genocide in 1994, with an estimated five hundred thousand to one million victims; the first and ongoing genocide of the twenty-first century, the Darfur genocide, with hundreds and thousands of victims and millions of displaced people; mass murders, lethal civil wars, and ethnic and religious strife that are going on in many parts of the world as I write these lines. Abject poverty on a grand scale dominates in large parts of the world, creating massive movements of fleeing populations who are seeking food and security in other lands. Would-be host countries react with anger and internal turmoil, the Left and the Right pitted against each other. All of this is happening on the watch of the United Nations, whose mission when it came into being after World War II was "to maintain international peace and security" — so far, a failed mission!

Tragically, we turned out to be wrong about social media. The hoped-for blessing — its potential role in spreading democracy and social equity — transformed into more of a curse. Holocaust denial started spreading widely in print form as early as 1969 by the far-right political activist Willis Carto, who advocated for a "racially pure" United States. But now, the internet and social media have allowed multiple supremacist ideologies (sometimes converging) to emerge, and revisionist websites, supposedly by historians, have cropped up, aiming to mislead unsuspecting, gullible and historically ignorant young students, and a good number of voting adults.

Few people, young or old, realize that Holocaust denial is one of the vilest forms of antisemitism and Jew-hatred — killing the victims twice. Countless Holocaust survivors, living eyewitnesses, have risen to the occasion and are still fighting back as public speakers. In person and through social media platforms, we try to educate students, teachers, politicians — anyone who will listen — about the historical truth through our personal stories. We are trying to explain how dangerous hate speech is if left unchallenged, how it leads to hateful and often lethal actions. We preach acceptance of diversity, inclusion, and human and civil rights for all in our still democratic, peaceful societies. We teach Holocaust history as a stern warning and as our best teacher, to convince today's generation not to repeat the enormous mistakes of that unprecedented, murderous period. Many young people have never heard of the Holocaust. It is vital to educate new generations about history in general and genocides in particular so that they are knowledgeable as they face a daily influx of information.

But our voices are not enough. The political leaders, with the backing of vibrant, engaged and enlightened civil societies, need to change the course of the conversation in communities that are developing divisive, ethnocentric, antagonistic and hateful cultures. Individually, each of us must help by making the decision every single day to fight discrimination and manifestations of hatred, and above all to remember that bad things happen when good people keep quiet.

~

Along with worrying about negative, frightening political and societal changes, our family faced a major health challenge in our private lives. About a year after we moved from our house into a condo, Sidney, then seventy years old, was diagnosed with Mild Cognitive Impairment (MCI) that signalled worrisome times ahead. The first five years after the diagnosis were spent strengthening Sid's memory capacity through the Baycrest Geriatric Centre's well-designed courses. We did travel though, when I was invited to the Bergen-Belsen Memorial Museum to an event at the new exhibition centre.

Sid still managed to swim forty laps daily, but sadly, his condition gradually slipped into dementia caused by Alzheimer's, with all its challenges, including deep bewilderment and heartache for our children and me. The impact of this long illness is beyond belief; our lives as we knew them until that point came to an end. The plans Sid and I had made for our "golden years" were dashed, and our family was in a state of paralysis as we witnessed Sid's decline, what people call "the long goodbye." For me, as his loving lifelong partner, the process was a deeply private, solitary struggle, a specific kind of solitude that was an ever-present loneliness. There was utter hopelessness in witnessing the daily effects of this cruel ailment on a once vibrant, mentally and physically active individual whom I loved and shared a lifetime bond with, but with whom I could no longer share even yesterday's happenings.

In the midst of writing this memoir, on July 11, 2019 at 6:45 a.m., after sixteen years of obliviousness and an intense twelve days of struggle, when he refused water and food, my beloved Sidney passed away. In some sense he had left us years ago; still, for a while I could hold his hands, play his favourite music, kiss his cheeks, comb his hair and talk to him. I felt I still belonged to him and he was still with me. I wasn't ready for the end and the enormous void he left behind — but it had to be endured. Jonathan's moving and remarkable eulogy illuminated the kind of outstanding man, husband and father he was. We will continue to miss Sidney's physical presence, but I am also left with an abundance of wonderful memories of him that will be a source of solace and will sustain us for years to come.

Afterword

I am now close to ninety-two years old, in failing health, coming rapidly to the end of *my* life and to the end of my story. Our children decided not to have children. What a pity. Or, looking at the world today, is it? Still, I would have loved to cuddle a few grandchildren, watch them grow up and see the continuity of the Weissenberg/ Cohen family.

Looking back on my life is very much like reliving it — a revised edition. Jotting down my memories has been a bittersweet, often traumatic but also happy endeavour. Could I, should I have left it unsaid, let it sink into oblivion? Not possible!

As the last survivor of my large family of yesteryear, it is my deeply felt obligation to remember and record the lives of all my beloved family members who once lived, worked and loved, but who were brutally murdered in a genocide just because they were Jews, and also to record it all for my children, Michelle and Jonathan.

It is imperative to talk about the tragic and intensely painful Holocaust experiences that forged me and my outlook on life, to record my experiences of how deeply intertwined the personal and the political were and are.

Now it is time to immerse myself in the varied, sometimes even humorous, aspects of what my life has been.

It is time to assess the difficult aftermath — the struggle to want to go on living and build a new life in an entirely new milieu on treasured memories and on the ruins of what remained.

It is time to truly appreciate the loving, lasting bond with my husband, our children and extended family.

It is time to take stock of my endeavours to contribute in a small but positive way to our civil society — especially an awareness that "women's rights are human rights," and that these rights need to be understood and respected.

It is time to look with open eyes and an open mind at the world as it is now, its magnificent progress — the many areas of development in technology, the arts, music, the sciences and humanities — but also its multipronged unsolved problems, its seemingly irreconcilable conflicts.

My generation is failing to tackle the urgent issues connected with climate change — to save the water, the air, the earth and the forests — and it has also failed to bring about a much-hoped-for global reconciliation.

The hope, of course, lies in knowing that we humans can also attain greatness in goodness. We know that caring for others and saving lives, even when facing great danger, has happened many times; there are shining precedents among the famous as well as among ordinary citizens during the Holocaust and World War II. They ought to be our role models.

The time has to come when future generations will search for and find the way to end this endless senseless hate and find common ground for the good of all humanity.

Glossary

aliyah (Hebrew; pl. *aliyot*, ascent) A term used by Jews and modern Israelis to refer to Jewish immigration to Israel; the term is also used to refer to "going up" to the altar in a synagogue to read from the Torah.

Allies The coalition of countries that fought against the Axis powers (Germany, Italy and Japan and later others). At the beginning of World War II in September 1939, the coalition included France, Poland and Britain. After Germany invaded the USSR in June 1941 and the United States entered the war following the bombing of Pearl Harbor by Japan on December 7, 1941, the main leaders of the Allied powers became Britain, the USSR and the United States. Other Allies included Canada, Australia, India, Greece, Mexico, Brazil, South Africa and China.

American Jewish Joint Distribution Committee (JDC) Colloquially known as the Joint, the JDC was a charitable organization founded in 1914 to provide humanitarian assistance and relief to Jews all over the world in times of crisis. It provided material support for persecuted Jews in Germany and other Nazi-occupied territories and facilitated their immigration to neutral countries such as Portugal, Turkey and China. Between 1939 and 1944, Joint officials helped close to 81,000 European Jews find asylum in various parts of the world. Between 1944 and 1947, the JDC assisted

more than 100,000 refugees living in DP camps by offering re-
training programs, cultural activities and financial assistance for
emigration.

Arrow Cross Party (in Hungarian, Nyilaskeresztes Párt — Hungaris-
ta Mozgalom; abbreviation: Nyilas) A Hungarian right-wing ex-
tremist and antisemitic party founded by Ferenc Szálasi in 1935 as
the Party of National Will. The newly renamed Arrow Cross Party
ran in Hungary's 1939 election and won 15 per cent of the vote. The
party was fought and largely suppressed by the regime in the coming years, but re-emerged as a major force in March 1944, when
Germany occupied Hungary; in August 1944, the party was temporarily banned. Under Nazi approval, the party, led by Szálasi,
assumed control of Hungary from October 15, 1944, to March 28,
1945. The Arrow Cross regime instigated the murder of tens of
thousands of Hungarian Jews. Starting on November 6, with the
last group leaving on December 11, 1944, approximately 70,000
Jews were rounded up and sent on death marches toward Greater
Germany. Tens of thousands died or were murdered along the
way, and some 50,000 survivors were handed over to the Germans. Between October 1944 and January 1945, the Arrow Cross
murdered thousands of Jews in Budapest.

Auschwitz (German; in Polish, Oświęcim) A Nazi concentration
camp complex in German-occupied Poland about 50 kilometres
from Krakow, on the outskirts of the town of Oświęcim, built between 1940 and 1942. The largest camp complex established by
the Nazis, Auschwitz contained three main camps: Auschwitz I, a
concentration camp; Auschwitz II (Birkenau), a death camp that
used gas chambers to commit mass murder; and Auschwitz III
(also called Monowitz or Buna), which provided slave labour for
an industrial complex. In 1942, the Nazis began to deport Jews
from almost every country in Europe to Auschwitz, where they
were selected for slave labour or for death in the gas chambers.
Starting in May 1944, over 420,000 Hungarian Jews were deported

to Auschwitz in mass transports, with smaller groups arriving through October 1944. The majority of these Jews were killed immediately in the gas chambers. In mid-January 1945, close to 60,000 inmates were sent on a death march, leaving behind only a few thousand inmates who were liberated by the Soviet army on January 27, 1945. It is estimated that 1.1 million people were murdered in Auschwitz, approximately 90 per cent of whom were Jewish; other victims included Polish prisoners, Roma and Soviet prisoners of war. *See also* Birkenau; death march.

Auschwitz-Birkenau *See* Auschwitz; Birkenau.

Austro-Hungarian Empire (also Austria-Hungary, the Dual Monarchy) The empire that united the Austrian Empire and the Kingdom of Hungary from 1867 to 1918. Responding to Hungary's desire for independence from the Hapsburg (also Habsburg) monarchy, Emperor Franz Joseph of Austria reached a compromise with Hungary, forming the Austro-Hungarian Empire. The two states remained independent, except for military and foreign affairs, and Franz Joseph ruled over the dual monarchy as emperor of Austria and king of Hungary. The presence of numerous ethnic groups within the empire, including Czechs, Slavs, Italians, Poles and Germans, weakened its power and led to the empire's dissolution after World War I, when the independent states of Czechoslovakia, Poland, Hungary, Austria and the State of Slovenes, Croats and Serbs (later Yugoslavia) were declared. *See also* Emperor Franz Joseph.

Axis alliance The coalition of countries that fought against the Allied powers (Britain, the United States, the USSR and others). At the beginning of World War II in September 1939, the coalition included Germany, Italy and Japan. Other Axis countries included Hungary, Romania, Slovakia, Bulgaria, Yugoslavia and Croatia.

BIIe / Gypsy family camp (in German, *Zigeunerfamilienlager*) The section of the Auschwitz-Birkenau death camp to which Roma families were transported starting in February 1943. When guards tried to liquidate the camp in May 1944, the inmates resisted and the liquidation was postponed. The camp was liquidated on August 2–3, 1944. Of the 23,000 Roma sent to Auschwitz-Birkenau, 20,000 were murdered. *See also* Auschwitz; Birkenau; Roma.

BIII / Mexico The third building sector designed to expand the Auschwitz-Birkenau death camp, called "Mexico" in camp jargon. Construction on the section began in mid-1943 with the aim of housing 60,000 inmates but was stopped in mid-1944 because of the approach of the Soviet army, with only 32 of a planned 188 barracks completed. There were no bathrooms in this sector and often no bunks in the barracks, and inmates sometimes had only scraps of rags and blankets as clothing. Hungarian women were transported to BIII starting in May 1944, after which there were transports from other countries, keeping the population of BIII above 10,000 during its existence. BIII was liquidated in October 1944, and remaining prisoners were sent to the women's section of Auschwitz-Birkenau. *See also* Auschwitz; Birkenau.

bar mitzvah (Hebrew; son of the commandment) The time when, in Jewish tradition, boys become religiously and morally responsible for their actions and are considered adults for the purpose of synagogue and other rituals. Traditionally this occurs at age thirteen for boys.

Beifeld, György (1902–1982; also George W. Byfield) A Hungarian Jew from Budapest who was conscripted into the Hungarian labour battalions and served on the Eastern Front from April 1942 through May 1943, after which he was taken to the Dachau concentration camp until liberation. While at the Eastern Front, Beifeld wrote about his experiences and created 402 drawings and watercolours. Beifeld's illustrated memoir, the Beifeld album, is notable for its detailed and humorous written and visual depictions of the events he witnessed. The album is currently housed at the United States Holocaust Memorial Museum. *See also* labour battalions.

Bergen-Belsen A concentration camp complex in Germany comprising three sections: a prisoner-of-war camp, established in 1940; a residence camp that held Jews who were to be exchanged for German nationals or goods, established in 1943; and a prisoners' camp, which held prisoners from other camps who were brought in to build the residence camp. The residence camp was divided into a number of groups, with different rules applying to each: The "star camp" was the largest group, holding about 4,000 "exchange Jews" who were all required to do manual labour; the "neutral camp," for Jews who were citizens of neutral countries, had better conditions and the inmates didn't work; the "special camp" held Polish Jews, most of whom were deported to Auschwitz; and the "Hungarian camp" held Hungarian Jews, some of whom were eventually released to Switzerland. Toward the end of the war, thousands of prisoners from camps close to the front lines were sent on death marches to Bergen-Belsen, pushing the number of inmates from about 15,000 in December 1944 to over 55,000 by April 1945, and causing a rapid deterioration in camp conditions. British forces liberated the camp on April 15, 1945. An estimated 50,000 people died in Bergen-Belsen.

Birkenau Also known as Auschwitz II. One of the camps in the Auschwitz complex in German-occupied Poland and the largest death camp established by the Nazis. Birkenau was built in 1941, and in 1942 the Nazis designated it as a killing centre, using Zyklon B gas to carry out the systematic murder of Jews and other people considered "undesirable" by the Nazis. In 1943, the Nazis began to use four crematoria with gas chambers that could hold up to 2,000 people each to murder the large numbers of Jews who were being brought to the camp from across Europe. Upon arrival, prisoners were selected for slave labour or sent to the gas chambers. The camp was liberated in January 1945 by the Soviet army. An estimated 1.1 million people were killed in the Auschwitz camp complex, most of them in Birkenau and the vast majority of them Jews. *See also* Auschwitz.

Borochov A socialist Zionist youth group based on the ideas of Ber Borochov (1881–1917), a Marxist Zionist theorist who was one of the founders of the Labour Zionist movement. *See also* Zionism.

Bricha (Hebrew; escape) The name given to the massive clandestine movement that organized the illegal migration of Jewish refugees from Eastern Europe to pre-state Israel after World War II. Estimates of the number of Jews who reached Palestine with Bricha range from 80,000 to 250,000. Although the goal of the organization was to smuggle Jews to pre-state Israel, some used the group and its connections to escape from Communist countries to displaced persons camps in Austria and Germany.

British Mandate Palestine (also Mandatory Palestine) The area of the Middle East under British rule from 1923 to 1948 comprising present-day Israel, Jordan, the West Bank and the Gaza Strip. The Mandate was established by the League of Nations after World War I and the collapse of the Ottoman Empire; the area was given to the British to administer until a Jewish national home could be established. During this time, Jewish immigration was severely restricted, and Jews and Arabs clashed with the British and each other as they struggled to realize their national interests. The Mandate ended on May 15, 1948, after the United Nations Partition Plan for Palestine was adopted and on the same day that the State of Israel was declared.

Canadian Jewish Congress (CJC) An advocacy organization and lobbying group for the Canadian Jewish community founded in 1919. The CJC was restructured in 2007 and its functions subsumed under the Centre for Israel and Jewish Affairs (CIJA) in 2011.

Central Committee of Liberated Jews The organization that represented Jewish displaced persons (DPs) in the British and American Zones of occupation after World War II. The committee set up departments to support all aspects of Jewish DP life, including education, health, culture, religion, emigration, family tracing and legal affairs. *See also* displaced persons (DP) camps.

challah (Hebrew) Braided egg bread traditionally eaten on the Jewish Sabbath as well as on other Jewish holidays. *See also* Shabbos.

chametz (Hebrew; leaven) Foods made from five grains — wheat, barley, spelt, oat or rye — that have been combined with water and allowed to rise or ferment. On the Jewish festival of Passover, *chametz* is not supposed to be consumed, owned or benefited from in any way. *See also* Passover.

Chanukah (also Hanukah; Hebrew; dedication) An eight-day festival of lights, usually celebrated in December, that commemorates the victory of the Jews against the Syrian-Greek empire in the second century BCE. The festival is celebrated with the lighting of an eight-branched candelabrum called a menorah, or chanukiyah, in remembrance of the rededication of the Temple in Jerusalem and the miracle of one day's worth of oil burning for eight days of light.

chanukiyah See Chanukah.

cholent (Yiddish) A traditional Jewish stew usually prepared on Friday and slow-cooked overnight to be eaten for Shabbat (the Sabbath) lunch. Ingredients for cholent vary by geographic region, but usually include meat, potatoes, beans and a grain. *See also* Shabbos.

Cold War The era of political hostility between the Soviet Union and the United States and their respective allies from the end of World War II until the fall of Eastern European Communist regimes in 1989. The Cold War era in America was characterized by a fear of Communist influences and the threat of imminent nuclear war.

death march A term that refers to the forced travel of prisoners who were evacuated from Nazi camps near the advancing military front to camps within Greater Germany in late 1944 and early 1945. Amid the chaos as the end of the war neared, the death marches prevented prisoners from being freed by liberating Allied armies and kept them under the Nazi regime to be used as slave labour for as long as possible. Prisoners often had to walk hundreds of kilometres under difficult conditions and at least

250,000 prisoners died of starvation, exhaustion, exposure, or at the hands of SS guards if they collapsed or could not keep up with others on the march.

denazification The effort by the Allied countries to eliminate the influence of Nazi ideology from postwar Germany by removing members of the National Socialist Party from public office and positions of influence.

displaced persons (DP) camps Facilities set up by the Allied authorities and the United Nations Relief and Rehabilitation Administration (UNRRA) in October 1945 to resolve the refugee crisis that arose at the end of World War II. The camps provided temporary shelter and assistance to the millions of people — not only Jews — who had been displaced from their home countries as a result of the war and helped them prepare for resettlement.

Eichmann, Adolf (1906–1962) The head of the Gestapo's Jewish Affairs department, which was responsible for the implementation of the Nazis' policy of mass murder of Jews. Eichmann was in charge of transporting Jews to death camps in Poland and coordinated deportations from Slovakia, the Netherlands, France, Belgium, Greece, northern Italy and Hungary. After the war, Eichmann escaped from US custody and fled to Argentina, where he was captured in 1960 by Israeli intelligence operatives; his ensuing 1961 trial in Israel was widely and internationally televised. Eichmann was sentenced to death and hanged in 1962.

Emperor Franz Joseph (1830–1916) Emperor of Austria (1848–1916) and King of Hungary (1867–1916). Franz Joseph created the dual monarchy in 1867, giving Hungary equal status within the new Austro-Hungarian Empire. His annexation of Bosnia and Herzegovina in 1908 provoked Serbian nationalists and led to the Archduke Franz Ferdinand's assassination and World War I. The Jewish population under the rule of Franz Joseph enjoyed a period of freedom, peace and prosperity, and in 1867, the emperor granted them full equality.

Garment Workers Scheme (Also known as the Tailor Project) A program to bring approximately 2,500 displaced persons from Europe to Canada after World War II. The plan was conceived by the Canadian garment industry, which was experiencing a shortage of workers, in partnership with the Canadian Jewish Congress and other Jewish organizations, as a way to advocate for more Jews and refugees in general to be allowed to enter the country in spite of Canada's restrictive immigration policies. Leaders in the garment industry agreed to hire garment workers on one-year contracts, while Jewish community organizations covered transport and housing expenses. It was the first time Canada opened its borders to a large number of refugees after World War II.

gendarmes (derived from French, *gens d'armes*, people of arms) Members of a military or paramilitary force, or gendarmerie, in France and, during World War II, in Hungary.

Grese, Irma (1923–1945) Also known as the Blond Angel of Auschwitz, the Beautiful Beast or the Bitch of Belsen. Grese was a notoriously sadistic female Nazi SS guard, trained in Ravensbrück in 1942 at the age of nineteen. Grese also served as an overseer, or *Aufseherin*, in Auschwitz-Birkenau. She was known for her brutal beatings and cruel treatment of prisoners. Grese was tried in the Bergen-Belsen war crimes trial in Lüneburg, Germany, and was executed in December 1945. *See also* Auschwitz; Bergen-Belsen; Birkenau.

Haggadah (Hebrew; telling) A book of readings that lays out the order of the Passover seder and recounts the biblical exodus from Egypt. *See also* Mah Nishtana; Passover; seder.

Hashomer Hatzair (Hebrew; The Youth Guard) A left-wing Zionist youth movement founded in Central Europe in the early twentieth century to prepare young Jews to become workers and farmers, and to establish kibbutzim — collective settlements — in the Land of Israel. Before World War II, there were 70,000 Hashomer Hatzair members worldwide, and many of those in Nazi-occupied territories led resistance activities in the ghettos and concentration camps or joined partisan groups in the forests. It is the oldest Zionist youth movement still in existence. *See also* Zionism.

Havdalah (Hebrew; separation) A Jewish ritual done at the end of the Sabbath and Jewish holidays, marking the separation between days of holiness and ordinary weekdays. During the Havdalah after the Sabbath, blessings are recited over a cup of wine, fragrant spices and a flame. *See also* Shabbos.

Heritage Front A Canadian white supremacist, neo-Nazi group founded in 1989. The group was active in Canada — including organizing white-power rock concerts and rallies, and disseminating a newspaper — until the mid-1990s, when several of its leaders were jailed for spreading hate messages and the group declined in popularity. The group disbanded in 2005, when one of its founders, Wolfgang Dröge, was killed.

hora An Israeli folk dance that is performed by a group in a circle and is traditionally danced on celebratory occasions.

Horthy, Miklós (1868–1957) The regent of Hungary during the interwar period and for much of World War II. Horthy presided over numerous governments that were aligned with the Axis powers and pursued antisemitic politics. After the German army occupied Hungary in March 1944, Horthy served primarily as a figurehead to the pro-Nazi government led by Döme Sztójay; nevertheless, he was able to order the suspension of the deportation of Hungarian Jews to death camps in the beginning of July 1944. Horthy planned to withdraw his country from the war on October 15, 1944, but the Nazis supported an Arrow Cross coup that same day and forced Horthy to abdicate. *See also* Arrow Cross Party.

International Ladies' Garment Workers' Union (ILGWU) A labour union in the United States and Canada that formed in New York City in 1900 to represent workers in the women's clothing industry. The ILGWU made significant advances in the rights of garment workers, improving working conditions and pay for its members. It merged with the Union of Needletrades, Industrial and Textile Employees in 1995.

International Refugee Organization (IRO) A temporary organization established in 1946 that became an agency of the United Nations to deal with the refugee crisis after World War II. It took on the functions of the United Nations Relief and Rehabilitation Administration (UNRRA) and was replaced by the Office of the High Commissioner for Refugees established in 1952 (now the United Nations High Commissioner for Refugees). The IRO resettled approximately one million displaced persons.

Jewish Relief Unit (JRU) A branch of the Jewish Committee for Relief Abroad, created in 1943 to provide relief and rehabilitation to refugees and Holocaust survivors. JRU was active in displaced person (DP) camps in Germany after the war until 1950.

Kaddish (Aramaic; holy. Also known as the Mourner's Kaddish or Mourner's Prayer.) The prayer recited by mourners at funerals and memorials and during Jewish prayer services. Kaddish is traditionally said by a relative of the deceased for eleven months after the death of a parent and for thirty days after the death of a spouse or sibling, as well as each year on the anniversary of the death.

kapo (German) A concentration camp prisoner appointed by the SS to supervise other prisoners in exchange for special privileges, like extra food or better sleeping arrangements. The kapos were often cruel to their fellow prisoners.

Kazet Concentration camp. The word "*Kazet*" is derived from the pronunciation of the German letters KZ, an abbreviation of *Konzentrationslager*, concentration camp.

kibbutz (Hebrew) A collectively owned farm or settlement in Israel, democratically governed by its members.

kosher (Hebrew) Fit to eat according to Jewish dietary laws. Observant Jews follow a system of rules known as *kashruth* that regulates what can be eaten, how food is prepared and how animals are slaughtered. Food is kosher when it has been deemed fit for consumption according to this system of rules. There are several foods that are forbidden, most notably pork products and shellfish.

Kotel (Hebrew; also Western Wall or Wailing Wall) A remnant of a wall from the Second Temple, the second ancient holy Jewish temple in Jerusalem, which was destroyed by the Romans in 70 CE. The Western Wall is considered the most sacred site in Judaism and is a place of prayer for Jews who visit from around the world.

Kristallnacht (German; Night of Broken Glass) A series of antisemitic attacks instigated by the Nazi leadership that were perpetrated in Germany and the recently annexed territories of Austria and the Sudetenland on November 9 and 10, 1938. During Kristallnacht, ninety-one Jews were murdered, and between 25,000 and 30,000 Jewish men were arrested and deported to concentration camps. More than two hundred synagogues were burned down, and thousands of Jewish homes and businesses were ransacked, their windows shattered, giving Kristallnacht its name. This attack is considered a decisive turning point in the Nazis' systematic persecution of Jews.

labour battalions (also referred to as auxiliary labour service, forced labour battalions or forced labour service) Units of Hungary's military-related labour service system (in Hungarian, *Munkaszolgálat*), which was first established in 1919 for those considered too "politically unreliable" for regular military service. After the labour service was made compulsory in 1939, Jewish men of military age were recruited to serve; however, having been deemed "unfit" to bear arms, they were equipped with tools and employed in mining, road and rail construction and maintenance work. Though the men were treated relatively well at first, the system became increasingly punitive. By 1941, Jews in forced labour battalions were required to wear an armband and civilian clothes; they had no formal rank and were unarmed; they were often mistreated by extremely antisemitic supervisors; and the work they had to do, such as clearing minefields, was often fatal. By 1942, 100,000 Jewish men had been drafted into labour battalions, and by the time the Germans occupied Hungary in March 1944, between 25,000 and 40,000 Hungarian Jewish men had died during their forced labour service.

Lager (German) Camp.

latke A fried potato patty traditionally eaten on the Jewish holiday of Chanukah. *See also* Chanukah.

Mah Nishtana (also the Four Questions) The questions that are recited at the start of the Passover seder, usually by the youngest child at the table. The questions revolve around the theme of how this night of commemoration of the Exodus from Egypt is different from other nights — e.g., Why do we eat unleavened bread? Why do we eat bitter herbs? The readings that follow answer the questions and in doing so tell the Exodus story. *See also* Passover; seder.

March of the Living An annual two-week program that takes place in Poland and Israel and aims to educate primarily Jewish students and young adults from around the world about the Holocaust and Jewish life before and during World War II. On Holocaust Memorial Day (Yom HaShoah), participants and Holocaust survivors march the three kilometres from Auschwitz to Birkenau to commemorate and honour all who perished in the Holocaust. Afterwards, participants travel to Israel and join in celebrations there for Israel's remembrance and independence days.

McCarthyism The era of American politics in the 1950s when US Senator Joseph McCarthy initiated investigations to expose Communist infiltration among members of the US government. McCarthy's allegations were never supported by proof but led to 2,000 government employees losing their jobs. The term is used generally to refer to the practice of making unsupported accusations of treason. *See also* Cold War.

Mengele, Josef (1911–1979) The most notorious of about thirty SS physicians in Auschwitz. Mengele was stationed at the camp from May 1943 to January 1945, first as the medical officer of the Birkenau "Gypsy camp" and later as chief medical officer of Birkenau. Mengele was one of the camp doctors responsible for deciding which prisoners were fit for slave labour and which were to be sent immediately to the gas chambers. He was also known for conducting sadistic experiments on Jewish and Roma prisoners, especially twins.

Mexico *See* B I I I.

mezuzah (Hebrew; doorpost) The small piece of parchment containing the text of the central Jewish prayer, the Shema, which has been handwritten in ink by a scribe. Many Jews place this parchment on the doorposts of their homes, often in decorative cases.

minyan (Hebrew; count, number) The quorum of ten adult Jews, traditionally male, required for certain religious rites. The term can also designate a congregation.

numerus clausus (Latin; closed number) A quota limiting admission to institutions or professions. In nineteenth- and twentieth-century Eastern Europe, Jews were frequently restricted from entering universities, professional associations and public administration.

Nyilas *See* Arrow Cross Party.

Organization for Rehabilitation through Training (ORT) A vocational school system founded for Jews by Jews in Russia in 1880 to promote economic self-sufficiency in impoverished communities. The name ORT derives from the acronym of the Russian organization Obshestvo Remeslenogo Zemledelcheskogo Truda, Society for Trades and Agricultural Labour. ORT schools continued to operate through World War II. After the war, ORT set up rehabilitation programs for the survivors, serving approximately 85,000 people in 78 DP camps in Germany. Today, ORT is a nonprofit organization that provides educational services to communities all over the world.

Orthodox (Judaism) The religious practice of Jews for whom the observance of Judaism is rooted in the traditional rabbinical interpretations of the biblical commandments. Orthodox Jewish practice is characterized by strict observance of Jewish law and tradition, such as the prohibition to work on the Sabbath and certain dietary restrictions.

Ostarbeiter (German; Eastern workers) Soviet and Polish slave labourers, mostly Ukrainians, who were forced to work to supply labour for the German war effort during World War II.

Passover (in Hebrew, Pesach) An eight-day Jewish festival that takes place in the spring and commemorates the exodus of the Israelite slaves from Egypt. The festival begins with a lavish ritual meal called a seder, during which the story of the Exodus is told through the reading of a Jewish text called the Haggadah. During Passover, Jews refrain from eating any leavened foods. The name of the festival refers to God's "passing over" the houses of the Jews and sparing their lives during the last of the ten plagues, when the first-born sons of Egyptians were killed by God.

Purim (Hebrew; lots) The Jewish holiday that celebrates the Jews' escape from annihilation in Persia. The Purim story recounts how Haman, advisor to the King of Persia, planned to rid Persia of Jews, and how Queen Esther and her cousin Mordecai foiled Haman's plot by convincing the king to save the Jews. During the Purim festivities, people dress up in costumes, feast, read the story of Purim and send gifts of food and money to those in need. *See also shalach manos.*

Red Cross A humanitarian organization founded in 1863 to protect the victims of war. During World War II, the Red Cross provided assistance to prisoners of war by distributing food parcels and monitoring the situation in POW camps and also provided medical attention to wounded soldiers and civilians. Today, in addition to the international body, the International Committee of the Red Cross (ICRC), there are national Red Cross and Red Crescent societies in almost every country in the world.

Reform (Judaism) (also known as Progressive Judaism, Liberal Judaism) A Jewish denomination that emerged in nineteenth-century Germany in response to Jewish emancipation and integration into secular culture. Reform Judaism focuses on adapting religious life to new social and political conditions, understanding Jewish law to be non-binding and emphasizing ethical and progressive elements of Jewish tradition and practice over ritual ones.

Rhineland A region in western Germany bordering France, Belgium, Luxembourg and the Netherlands that was demilitarized as part of the peace treaties following World War I. In 1936, Hitler ordered German troops into the region, but faced no consequences for this violation of international treaties.

Roma (singular male, Rom; singular female, Romni) A traditionally itinerant ethnic group originally from northern India and primarily located in Central and Eastern Europe. The Roma, who have been referred to pejoratively as Gypsies, have often lived on the fringes of society and been subject to persecution. During the Holocaust, which the Roma refer to as the Porajmos — the destruction or devouring — Roma were stripped of their citizenship under the Nuremberg Laws and were targeted for death under Hitler's race policies. It is estimated that between 220,000 and 500,000 Roma were murdered in the Holocaust. Roma Holocaust Memorial Day is commemorated on August 2.

Rosh Hashanah (Hebrew; New Year) The two-day autumn holiday that marks the beginning of the Jewish year and ushers in the High Holy Days. It is celebrated with a prayer service and the blowing of the shofar (ram's horn), as well as festive meals that include symbolic foods such as an apple dipped in honey, which symbolizes the desire for a sweet new year.

schmaltz (Yiddish) Clarified chicken or goose fat used in Eastern European dishes for frying or spreading.

seder (Hebrew; order) A ritual meal celebrated at the beginning of the festival of Passover. A traditional seder involves reading the

Haggadah, which tells the story of the Israelite slaves' exodus from Egypt; drinking four cups of wine; eating matzah and other symbolic foods that are arranged on a special seder plate; partaking in a festive meal; and singing traditional songs. *See also* Passover.

Shabbos (Yiddish; Sabbath) The weekly day of rest beginning Friday at sunset and ending Saturday at nightfall, ushered in by the lighting of candles on Friday evening and the recitation of blessings over wine and challah (egg bread). A day of celebration as well as prayer, it is customary to eat three festive meals, attend synagogue services and refrain from doing any work or travelling.

shalach manos (Yiddish; in Hebrew, *mishloach manot*; sending of portions) A gift of food sent on the holiday of Purim. The tradition is sourced in the Book of Esther and is meant to bring people together and ensure that all members of the community can celebrate the holiday. *See also* Purim.

shoichet (Yiddish; in Hebrew, *shochet*, ritual slaughterer) A Jewish man trained to slaughter cattle and poultry so that it is fit to eat according to Jewish law.

shtetl (Yiddish) A mostly Jewish market town in Eastern Europe before World War II. Life in the shtetl revolved around Judaism and Jewish culture and was defined by the closely intertwined economic and social lives of its residents. Shtetls existed in Eastern Europe from the sixteenth century until they were wiped out in the Holocaust.

siddur (Hebrew) A Jewish prayer book.

Star of David (in Hebrew, *Magen David*) The six-pointed star that is the most recognizable symbol of Judaism. During World War II, Jews in Nazi-occupied areas were frequently forced to wear a badge or armband with the Star of David on it as an identifying mark of their lesser status and to single them out as targets for persecution.

Stutthof A concentration camp established on September 2, 1939, near Danzig (Gdańsk), Poland. Initially its inmates were predominantly Poles, though the camp population also included Jews, political prisoners, criminals and others. In the late summer of 1944, tens of thousands of Jews arrived from the ghettos in the Baltic States and Poland, as well as from Hungary via Auschwitz, and the population of the camp became predominantly Jewish. Altogether, Stutthof held around 110,000 prisoners, of which at least 65,000 died from overwork, disease, malnutrition, abuse and, especially toward the end of the war, lethal injection or gas. On January 25, 1945, 11,000 of the 50,000 camp inmates were forced on a death march. The survivors of the march were interned in a temporary camp and were liberated at the beginning of March 1945. Many who remained behind in Stutthof died from hunger or typhus, or as a result of further evacuations and mass executions. One hundred inmates of Stutthof were liberated by Soviet forces on May 9, 1945.

Sudetenland The name used between 1919 and the end of World War II to refer to the region of Czechoslovakia that bordered on Germany and Austria and was inhabited primarily by ethnic Germans. The Sudetenland was annexed by Germany in October 1938 under the terms of the Munich Agreement.

sukkah See Sukkot.

Sukkot (Hebrew; Feast of Tabernacles) An autumn harvest festival that recalls the forty years during which the ancient Israelites wandered in the desert after their exodus from slavery in Egypt. The holiday lasts for seven days, during which Jews traditionally eat meals in a *sukkah*, a temporary structure covered with a roof made from leaves or branches.

Sztójay, Döme (1883–1946) Prime minister of Hungary from March 22, 1944, to August 29, 1944. A former general in the Hungarian army and Hungarian ambassador to Germany from 1935 to 1944, Sztójay had strong ties to Nazi Germany and played a pivotal role in the mass deportations of Hungarian Jews during his time as prime minister. After the war, Sztójay was found guilty of war crimes and executed in 1946 in Budapest.

Torah scroll (in Hebrew, Sefer Torah) A scroll of parchment containing the text of the Torah, specifically the Five Books of Moses (the first books of the Hebrew Bible), the content of which is traditionally believed to have been revealed to Moses at Mount Sinai. The Torah scroll is handwritten by a trained scribe with ink and a quill and is covered with a decorative mantel or case and with silver or gold ornaments. The scroll is used for Torah readings and prayers in synagogues, where it is housed in a special ark and treated with great respect.

Totenkopfverbäende (German; Death's Head units) SS units that served as guards in Nazi camps and in combat during World War II, known for their brutality. A skull-and-crossbones insignia was displayed on the collars of their uniforms.

Treaty of Trianon One of the five treaties produced at the 1919 Paris Peace Conference organized by the victors of World War I. The Treaty of Trianon, signed in 1920, imposed a harsh peace on Hungary, newly independent from the dissolved Austro-Hungarian Empire, exacting reparations and redrawing its borders so that Hungary lost over two-thirds of its territory and more than half of its inhabitants.

United Jewish Peoples' Order (UJPO) A secular socialist Jewish organization in Canada founded in 1926 that sponsors educational and cultural programming.

United Nations Relief and Rehabilitation Administration (UNRRA) An international relief agency created at a 44-nation conference in Washington, DC, on November 9, 1943, to provide economic assistance and basic necessities to war refugees. It was especially active in repatriating and assisting refugees in the formerly Nazi-occupied European nations immediately after World War II.

Yad Vashem Israel's official Holocaust memorial centre and the world's largest collection of information on the Holocaust, established in

1953. Yad Vashem, the World Holocaust Remembrance Center, is dedicated to commemoration, research, documentation and education about the Holocaust. The Yad Vashem complex in Jerusalem includes museums, sculptures, exhibitions, research centres and the Garden of the Righteous Among the Nations.

yeshiva (Hebrew) A Jewish educational institution in which religious texts such as the Torah and Talmud are studied.

Yom Kippur (Hebrew; Day of Atonement) A solemn day of fasting and repentance that comes eight days after Rosh Hashanah, the Jewish New Year, and marks the end of the High Holidays.

Zionism A movement promoted by the Viennese Jewish journalist Theodor Herzl, who argued in his 1896 book *Der Judenstaat* (The Jewish State) that the best way to resolve the problem of antisemitism and persecution of Jews in Europe was to create an independent Jewish state in the historical Jewish homeland of biblical Israel. Zionists also promoted the revival of Hebrew as a Jewish national language.

Photographs

1 Judy's parents, Margit and Sándor Weissenberg. Debrecen, Hungary, 1910.
2 Judy (far right) and her sisters Évi (left) and Klári (centre). Debrecen, circa 1933.

Judy (seated, right) with siblings and her cousin. Standing (left to right): Klári, Laci and Évi. In front: Judy's cousin, name unknown (left) and Judy (right). Debrecen, circa 1931.

1 Judy's brother Jenö with his wife, Magda, on their wedding day. Debrecen, 1930s. Courtesy of the Neuberger Holocaust Education Centre.

2 Judy's sister Böske (Erzsébet), just after graduating high school. Debrecen, 1933.

3 Judy's brother Miklós. Debrecen, circa 1935.

4 Judy's sister Klári (left) with her best friend, Elizabeth Neumann. Debrecen, circa 1937.

1

2

1 Judy (back row, fourth from the left) with her middle-school class. Judy's best
  friend, Agi Losonczi, is on Judy's right, and her "camp sister" Edit Feig is sitting
  in the first row on the left. Debrecen, circa 1940.

2 From left to right: Judy's sisters Évi and Klári; Judy's father, Sándor; and Judy.
  Debrecen, circa 1943.

KL BUCHENWALD   (Frauen)   T/D Nr. | 4 | 0 | 1 | 1 | 4 | 3 |

FEIG,
NAME   Judith
       Vorname

17.9.28   Debreczen   63082
Geb.-Datum   Geb.-Ort   Häftl.-Nr.

Häftl. Pers. Karte . . . . ☐   Mil. Gov. Quest. . . . . ☐
Frauenkarte 1 u. 2 . . . ☐   Order f. Disp . . . . . . ☐
Effektenkarte . . . . . . ☑   Todesmeldung . . . . ☐
Postkontr.-Karte . . . . ☐   Soz. Vers. Unterlagen . . ☐
Schreibst.-Karte . . . . ☐
Häftl. Pers. Bogen . . . . ☑
Revierkarte . . . . . . ☐
Krankenblätter . . . . . ☐
Arbeitskarte . . . . . . ☑
Geldverw.-Karte . . . . ☐
Nummernkarte . . . . . ☐

Dokumente: 3
Inf. Karten:
Bemerkungen:

Umschlag Nr.:   5043

1

Junkus – Aschersleben
(63.001 – 64.000)   56

Datum	Zugang	Abgang	Im/nach	Liste Nummer	Bestand
2.1.45	500		Berg-Belsen 23.1.45		500
18.1.45		1	63.473 Weiss, Bouska		499
16.2.45		1	63.054 Danzig, Sabine		498
20.2.45		1	63.220 Knopf, Rela		497
14.3.45		1	63.463 Wojs, Hela, Esma		496
19.3.45		1	63.025 Birnbaum, Minna		495

2

1   Judy's prisoner card from the Aschersleben slave labour camp, a subcamp of
Buchenwald, where she was sent in January 1945.

2   A handwritten document recording the arrival and registration of 500 women
from Bergen-Belsen to Aschersleben in January 1945. Judy was on this transport.
Courtesy of Arolsen Archives.

1 Judy with her friends. From left to right: Judy, Anci Weiss and Agi Losonczi. Debrecen, 1945.
2 Judy's brother Laci (Leslie), after the war. Hungary, 1946.
3 Judy with Chaver Steiner at the ORT dental technical school in the Bergen-Belsen DP camp. Germany, circa 1947.

1 Judy at work with Chaver Rosenberg at the ORT dental technical school in the Bergen-Belsen DP camp. Circa 1947.

2 Judy with her ORT Dental Technical School class in the Bergen-Belsen DP camp. Judy is sitting on the left in the second row from the bottom. Circa 1947.

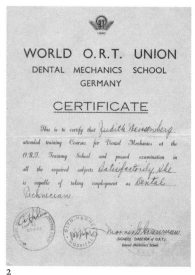

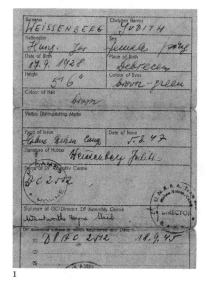

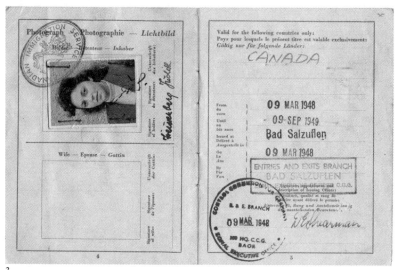

1 Judy's displaced persons identification card.

2 Judy's certificate of completion of her dental technician training at the ORT school at the Bergen-Belsen DP camp. Courtesy of Bergen-Belsen archives.

3 Judy's DP passport, a temporary travel document issued in lieu of a passport for stateless persons of undetermined nationality. Courtesy of Bergen-Belsen archives.

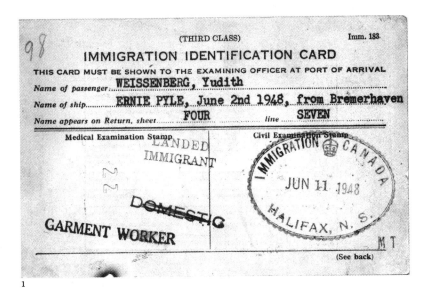

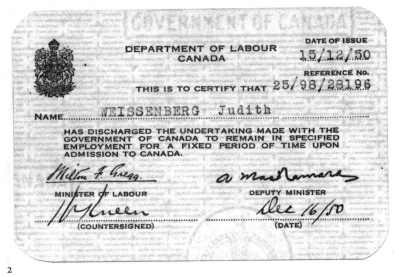

1 Judy's immigration identification card. Courtesy of the Neuberger Holocaust Education Centre.

2 Certificate from the Department of Labour Canada to certify that Judy fulfilled her work obligations as an immigrant to the country. Courtesy of the Neuberger Holocaust Education Centre.

1 Judy in her first winter coat and boots. Montreal, 1948.
2 Judy, sitting on the hood of the car on the right, and her sister Évi, sitting on the hood of the car on the left, with their friends. Montreal, 1948.
3 Judy and her husband, Sidney Cohen, signing their marriage contract. Montreal, June 9, 1961.
4 Judy and Sidney dancing to violin music played by close friend Sam Balderman at their wedding. Montreal, June 9, 1961.

Judy and her husband, Sidney Cohen, on their wedding day. Montreal, June 9, 1961.

1 Judy's sister Évi. Montreal, 1960s.
2 Judy's brother Leslie (Laci). Toronto, 1972.
3 Judy (centre) with her "camp sisters," Edit (left) and Sári (right). Montreal, 1989.

1   Judy (centre) with her husband, Sidney (front), her daughter, Michelle, and her
son, Jonathan. Toronto, 1980s.

2   Judy's daughter, Michelle. Toronto, circa 1990.

3   Judy's son, Jonathan. Toronto, 2003.

1 Judy and Sidney in their garden. Toronto, circa 2000.
2 Judy and Sidney on a trip to Israel in 2005.

1

2

1 Judy addressing Canadian March of the Living participants at Auschwitz-Birkenau on Yom Hashoah, May 4, 1997. Photo by Elan Sloim.

2 Judy receiving the University of Toronto's Principal's Award from the University of Toronto Mississauga in recognition of her work in Holocaust education. Toronto, 2017. Photo by Blake Eligh.

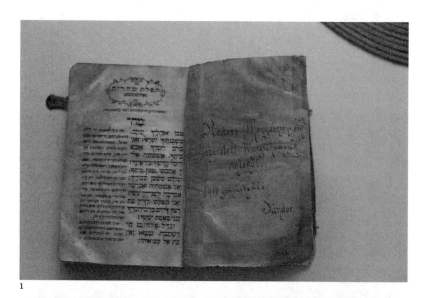

1

2

1 Judy's mother's prayer book, which is inscribed by Judy's father to her mother in honour of their wedding day. The prayer book was buried during the war. The inscription reads, "For my dear bride, my beloved Margit, a momento. June 22, 1910. Sándor."

2 A silver salt or sugar holder (left), engraved to Judy's parents as a wedding gift, dated June 10, 1910, and Judy's uncle's snuff holder (front, centre), among other silver items that belonged to Judy's family and were hidden during the war.

[This page and the following verso] Several awards that Judy received for her work in the community and for Holocaust education.

Judy Weissenberg Cohen. Toronto, 2017. Photo by Blake Eligh.

Index